COMMEMORATION BOOK
1914-19

With sorrowful hearts, but with a mighty pride, this book is reverently dedicated to all our Yorkshire players who have played "The Great Game"

Yorkshire Rugby Football Union

Commemoration Book
1914-19

The Naval & Military Press Ltd

Published by

The Naval & Military Press Ltd
Unit 5 Riverside, Brambleside
Bellbrook Industrial Estate
Uckfield, East Sussex
TN22 1QQ England

Tel: +44 (0)1825 749494

www.naval-military-press.com
www.nmarchive.com

In reprinting in facsimile from the original, any imperfections are inevitably reproduced and the quality may fall short of modern type and cartographic standards.

LIEUT.-COL. J. L. HICKSON J.P.
President of the Yorkshire Rugby Football Union

The Great War
1914-1919

THE GREAT WAR

On August 13th, 1914, the Rugby Football Union issued the following circular letter to all their clubs—

The Rugby Union are glad to know that a large number of their players have already volunteered for service.

They express a hope that all Rugby players will join some Force in their own town or county.

C. J. B. MARRIOTT, *Secretary*

On August 31st, 1914, the Yorkshire Rugby Union, at their first monthly meeting after war was declared, issued the following letter to all their clubs—

Below I beg to give you copy of resolution unanimously passed at meeting of the County Committee this evening. " That this Committee recommend that all football in the county be suspended during the continuance of the war, and we strongly appeal to our players to join some unit for the defence of the country.

" The Yorkshire Union confidently believe that every eligible player of theirs will place himself at the disposal of his country at this crisis."

R. F. OAKES, *Hon. Sec.*

Immediately after war was declared, a strong wish was expressed by Rugby men to form a " Rugby Union Footballer's Battalion," and representations were made to the Army Authorities to this effect.

On September 9th, 1914, the Rugby Union issued the following—

RUGBY FOOTBALL UNION AND LORD KITCHENER'S ARMY.

DEAR SIR,—On reference to the authorities, the Rugby Football Union find it is not feasible to form a separate battalion of Rugby men. They have received, however, answers from various Commanding Officers, saying that they will gladly accept for their Regiments a company about (120) of Rugby men, who could be enlisted together.

A very large number of our players have already responded to the previous letter of my Committee and joined some Corps, but it is probable there may be some others ready to enlist.

I will therefore enter names sent in to me, and as soon as I have enrolled sufficient to form a company, will send them on to a Commanding Officer for enlistment as a Football Company in Lord Kitchener's Army.

Applicants should state—
    (1) Football club.
    (2) Age.
    (3) Whether married or single.
    (4) Previous training (if any).

As previously announced, the Rugby Union have cancelled all their matches for this season.

Yours faithfully

C. J. B. MARRIOTT, *Secretary*

On September 16th, 1914, the following letter was addressed to all the clubs in the Union by the Yorkshire Rugby Union Committee—

At the request of the Committee of the above Union, I beg to hand you copy of circular letter issued by the Rugby Union (*Circular dated 9th September*).

It is hardly necessary to say that the Yorkshire Union very strongly support the suggestion of the Rugby Union, and beg of you to use every endeavour to put same before the players and members of your club.

It is the strong feeling of the Yorkshire Union that a vigorous attempt be made by all our clubs to get into touch, not only with their own members, who, for legitimate reasons, cannot join Lord Kitchener's Army, but with every boy in their town up to the age of 19, and man over the age of 35, with the object of forming a company in connection with your club, for the purposes of drilling and training in rifle practice.

There would probably be little or no difficulty in enlisting the services and sympathy of an ex-army man to act as instructor, and your own football ground could be utilised for drilling.

A course of drilling and instruction could be given, say, two or three nights a week and also on Saturday afternoons.

The Y.R.U. feel sure that it only requires publicity for an object like this to meet with a ready and hearty response.

It is the bounden duty of every man and boy at this critical stage in the history of our country to submit himself to some form of drilling and training, in order to fit himself to help defend his country, and no excuse ought to be tolerated for his non-compliance.

The Y.R.U. suggest that you, as secretary, should circularise any likely volunteer to the above object. Any reasonable expense in connection with circulars and postage would be gladly defrayed by the Y.R.U.

Kindly give this matter your prompt and earnest attention.

The Y.R.U. would be greatly obliged if you will please report, within the next fortnight, what progress you are making, so that any matter affecting the scheme can be dealt with at the meeting of the Committee on the 28th inst.

NO EFFORT can be too great to uphold our King and Country.

The Yorkshire Rugby Union feel justly proud of the magnificent response their players have made to the "Call to Arms."

It is their desire to obtain the names of all their players who have joined the Colours, either as regulars or territorials.

Will you therefore kindly prepare a list of your players, together with their rank and regiment, and let me have same in the course of the next fortnight, and oblige,

Yours faithfully

R. F. OAKES, *Hon. Secretary*

Copy of Minute passed at meeting of the Yorkshire Rugby Union, 31st August, 1914—

Decided unanimously to give £100 as a First Donation to the Prince of Wales' Relief Fund.

Copy of Minute passed at meeting of the Yorkshire Rugby Union, 12th October, 1914—

That a donation of 50 guineas be given by this Union to " The Belgian Relief Fund " now being raised in London, same to be remitted through the Local Secretary of the Fund, Mr. A. B. Balfour, Leeds.

Copy of Minute passed at meeting of the Yorkshire Rugby Union on 26th April, 1915—

The President (J. L. Hickson) spoke very feelingly of the truly magnificent response the Rugby Union men of Yorkshire had made to the call of King and Country.

It was impossible at the moment to obtain absolutely accurate information as to the total number of players who had joined the Colours, but it was a well-known fact that the great bulk had joined up immediately war was declared.

The President felt strongly that these facts be recorded on the Minutes of the Committee, as every Rugby lover was justifiably proud of the splendid way the Yorkshire Rugby Union players had responded to the " great call."

THE PRICE OF VICTORY

Up to the Armistice being signed the casualties were as follows—

BRITISH	Killed (Officers and Men)	658,704
	Wounded do.	2,032,142
	Missing and Prisoners	359,145
	Total	3,049,991
	Merchant Marines, Loss of Life	14,661
	Do. Captured and Detained	3,295
		3,067,947
	Royal Navy, &c.—Killed	33,361
	Wounded	5,183
	Missing and Prisoners	1,222
		3,107,713
FRANCE	Killed	1,071,300
	Prisoners and Missing	760,300
ITALY	Killed	460,000
	Wounded	946,990
AMERICA	Killed	53,169
	Wounded and Prisoners, &c.	152,948
RUSSIA	Killed	1,600,000
	Other Casualties	7,400,000
GERMANY	Killed	1,580,000
	Wounded	4,000,000
	Prisoners and Missing	750,000
AUSTRIA	Killed	800,000
	Other Casualties	3,200,000

When the figures for Roumania, Serbia, Belgium, Greece, and Turkey are added it is estimated that not less than ten million lives have been sacrificed, and those mostly the lives of valuable youth.

WAR BILL

Allies	£20,450,000,000
Foes	£10,250,000,000
Total	£30,700,000,000

It is estimated that Germany could pay out of her resources £30,000,000,000 by 1930.

A few Appreciations by some of those who have been intimately connected with the Rugby man

By Lieut.-Col. J. L. HICKSON J.P.
President Yorkshire Rugby Union

The idea of commemorating the supreme sacrifice made by so many of our Rugby Union players in the great war by the medium of a Book of Reference appeals to me as very well conceived. I do not think it would be easy to devise a better, or more lasting memento, and I am proud to pay my own tribute to our heroes, amongst the introductory notices which accompany these pages. Many of the dead and gone players were personally known to me, and if I said that I should miss them during the ensuing season, a trite expression of that kind could not convey my sense of loss by any means. It is, however, the Sport itself that suffers most by war's dreadful demand, and I can only hope that worthy successors to those now memorialised will, in course of time, be found carrying-on the ancient and glorious game of Rugby football. In this way we shall perhaps best demonstrate our respect, admiration, and affection for the brave boys who found their goal on the battle-fields of France, Belgium, and other countries.

J. L. Hickson

Bolton Grange
Bradford

By Alderman ARTHUR HARTLEY C.A. J.P.
President of the English Rugby Union and Hon. Treasurer of the Yorkshire Rugby Union

---

"How sleep the brave who sink to rest,
By all their country's wishes blest."

THE fierce fight for humanity is ended and once again peace reigns. But victory has been very hardly won, and its cost is not yet fully realised. True it is, however, that the great war has enabled us to discover the heroic splendour of our youth.

This development of the noblest qualities in the flower of our race is far from being put forward as any justification for war, but it cannot be denied that it is one of its sustaining consolations. The war has indeed shown of what our youth is capable. Times without number it has been noticed that the finest and purest kind of courage has been displayed by men of diverse parts and various characteristics.

One and all poured their gifts in a splendid stream to swell the great river of world effort. None held back—and least of all the " Rugger " men of this mighty Empire. The game was played " all in " until the final goal had been achieved. Alas! too many were the casualties of the great grim struggle. Many are gone never to return.

We mourn them; yet why mourn? Are not the departed among the glorious dead, to whose memory has been erected a lasting memorial in the hearts of those who will cherish the memory of their gallantry in the game and their chivalry in the battle for civilisation.

*　　*　　*　　*　•

Turning from our Empire outlook to our own native County, we find its record is one of which we may be justifiably proud. The names of more than 300 of its playing members are to be found on the roll of fame.

The esteem and pride of Yorkshiremen and others in the Rugby game has been shown to be well founded. The record of Yorkshire football is not merely one of great achievement. There is something greater than this—their spirit of fairness, unselfishness, and keenness.; their resource and grit. Yorkshire football has had its hard times as well as its good. Our defeats and our victories stand side by side. But win or lose, we pride ourselves that we have always played the game.

We are proud of the race that gave us Rugby football at its best, and we would hold to the fine traditions now handed down to us by the fallen, whose names are writ large in the annals of the Yorkshire Rugby Union. These traditions we must not only preserve, but pass on to the generation now succeeding. What of the men who will don the White Rose badge ? Will they live and play in such a spirit as to be worthy of their glorious predecessors ?

* * * *

Those who have gone must not be forgotten. Their memory must never grow dim. Their fineness of spirit and the manliness they displayed at the call of duty ! Their dreams and hopes for the future of mankind !

* * * *

Their supreme sacrifice will not have been in vain if we live nobly and carry into the game their spirit—not for self, but for the side ; not for the individual, but for the cause.

> " In grateful love I bow the knee,
> For nameless men who died for me."

Arthur Hartley

By G. ROWLAND HILL Esq.
Past President and Past Honorary Secretary of the English Rugby Union

THE RUGBY MAN

" And us they trusted ; we the task inherit,
The unfinished task for which their lives were spent ;
But leaving us a portion of their spirit,
They gave their witness and they died content."

I HOLD that an honour is doubly valued when it is conferred on a man by those whom he himself especially honours. Of such a one I have been a recipient when I am asked in the name of the Rugby footballers of Yorkshire to lay, so to speak, a wreath at the foot of the monument which they are erecting to the memory of their glorious dead. This expression is figurative, for the Yorkshiremen have chosen a book as their form of commemoration. Regarding books, one poet has said of his own—

" I have erected a monument more lasting than brass,"
and another—
" Not marble nor the gilded monuments
Of princes shall outlive this powerful rhyme,"
and surely we may hope that this sentiment may prove true of the work to which these lines are a feeble contribution. We may well expect that in the distant future this volume will be a treasured possession in many a Yorkshire home, and young children, relatives or descendants of those recorded in it, learn to point with pride and awe to the names of their heroic ancestors.

But when I come myself to write of the fame of these men, dead so young, dying so nobly, I must confess that my mind refuses to put into form the utterance of the feelings that lie in the depth of my heart. I must own that I can scarcely speak of them without a quavering of the voice, nor can I read of the simple inscriptions to their memory on tablets and tombs in our churches without tears gathering in my eyes. In the early days of the war, having to speak at a football meeting, I drew attention to the fact that several well known veteran Rugby players, whose names I gave, were at the time taking sentry duty at Buckingham Palace. A younger generation beyond the duty of guarding the person of the King was called to the plains of France and Flanders, to Gallipoli, Syria, and Mesopotamia, to maintain his honour, to uphold the repute and might of his Empire, and to defend the liberties of the Nations. On those plains the " muddied oafs " showed themselves fit compeers of the " Old Contemptibles." They went there "to do or to die, while all the world wondered." When I was a boy, in my spare winter hours, I played football simply because to me it was the right thing to do. I obeyed an instinct, if not of mankind, at least of our race. By doing so I feel convinced that I gained to myself a pure and ennobling delight. I am also sure that this is the case with true lovers of the game. In like manner our players, at the call of their Country, joined up in ungrudging cheerfulness simply because to them it was the right thing to do, and they have gained to themselves a good report. Perhaps of all the varying emotions which overwhelm our spirit in the contemplation of their fate and of their glory, the first place ought to be given to a holy unreserved reverence. Their careers answer to the tests by which Ruskin discerns the rightful objects of that feeling. Their motives were pure ; their bearing bright ; when tried in trench or combat they proved true ; they were gracious in their lives and great in their deaths ; their achievements were marvellous.

" They brake the jaws of the unrighteous and plucked the prey out of his teeth." " They played the game." This motto is now entering on a mellow old age. I note that it is coming to be appropriated on all sides. It is to be found in the orations of politicians and even in the sermons of preachers. But I believe that its early days were passed on the lips of followers of our game. I know that in my more active days in the last quarter of the nineteenth century I employed it often at football gatherings when urging my hearers to uphold the best traditions of the Rugby game. It must bring a certain amount of contentment to the band of brothers who at that period devoted no small amount of time and of energy to the furtherance of " Our Game," that the principles bound up in the very structure of it have inspired actions unparalleled in the history of the world.

By J. A. MILLER Esq.

I AM proud to add a tribute to the boys to whose memory this book is dedicated, but I feel that no words which I can express will get down to the depths of the admiration and respect I feel for them.

There is something touching, something that fascinates the imagination, in the spirit of patriotism, duty, and sacrifice shown by these boys in 1914, right down throughout the war. And what deeds of heroism, unknown, untold, are wrapped in the mystery of their end. Who knows?

This spirit was awakened when war was declared. It roused them when the old " contemptibles " rolled back from Mons. It grew in them until it became invincible, and nothing could satisfy it but Victory. Truly a wonderful, a magnificent spirit. It pointed to duty; they saw it; they did it; and when the cry rang out for men, they did not wait; they did not follow; but afraid of being left out of things, if too late, they gave themselves at once. Their Country needed them to uphold its cause of honour, right, and freedom, and that was enough!

Events moved rapidly in those days—a station; a hand clasp; " All's well, dad "; " Keep up, little girl "; " Goodbye, kid "; " Cheerio everybody "; a whistle; and they were gone. Au Revoir!

Time blurs the past, but can we forget? No!

Those who knew them can easily follow and picture them through all the time of their service, and feel sure

They played the game—all through.

From home and comfort they went to hardship, willingly and without a murmur. They toiled through the discipline and drudgery of training cheerfully, knowing they were paving the way to greater things.

But the time tried their patience, for their only wish was to be " out there "—in the greater game—" Somewhere "—doing their bit—their best—for England.

At length came the order " to go " ; a hasty leave—and they were off and reached the " Somewhere " of their wishes.

Their eyes opened to the reality of things, and with no illusions as to the frightfulness and fury of it all, they did not repine. The bull-dog courage of their race gripped them, and they held on.

And then, in the rotation of trenches and billets, came the moment when they had to take their chance " over the top." With pulses quickened they waited through the night, their minds filled with the hidden fear, but no regret. For the same spirit possessed them, strengthened them, uplifted them, until, as the dawn arose and the signal was given, it carried them over and on through the blinding showers of lead, until one, then another, and another, and more and yet more of them, called to the sacrifice, passed over into the shadows of the " Beyond."

Heroes ! Victims of a world's tragedy. So young ; so brave ; so great ; the manliest ; the best. One salutes them in silent reverence.

May the hand of the years beautify their memory.

J. A. MILLER

Headingley, Leeds

BY CAPTAIN THE REVEREND R. HUGGARD M.A. M.B.E.

THIS book, beautiful as it is, would not be complete without a word from some of those who have been closely associated with the heroes whose names are here recorded. As one of those thus associated, I have been asked to write a word of appreciation. To do this, I deem one of the highest honours I have ever experienced. I have worked with, I have played, yes, and have prayed with Rugger men for now upwards of thirty years—Englishmen, Scotchmen, Irishmen, Welshmen, and Colonials—all of them men in the truest sense of the word; virile, versatile, valiant, and venturesome. An Irishman myself, I have learned to trust and love Yorkshire Rugger men. During the past twenty years my life has been bound up with Yorkshire, and I can truly say that there is no finer sportsman living than the Yorkshireman. Like all Rugger men, they play the game. And what they have done on the field of play they have also done on the greater field of battle. When the war broke out, in August, 1914, Rugger men throughout the British Empire eagerly rushed to their Country's aid; nay, it was not merely Country, but Humanity. Clubs were forgotten, captains, secretaries, committeemen, players cast aside their "Rugger togs" and donned their Country's colours. It was no longer the pleasant piping of the whistle, no longer the captain's cry, "Play up and play to the whistle," which stirred the player to his best exertions, but now his ear is attuned to other sounds—the stern and decided word of command, the rattle of the rifle, the screaming of the machine gun fire, the bursting of the cannon.

Our heroes answered the call, they obeyed the command, they faced the deadly lead, the suffocating gas, the liquid fire; they never flinched. Some joined the Senior Service, and here also the same heroism was shown—whether on dreadnought or cruiser, on destroyer or submarine, keeping lonely vigil in the North Sea or chasing the more venturesome of enemy craft—our men were ever ready. The same spirit which helped them to play the game on land helped them when they rode the mighty deep or soared above the clouds. Yorkshire may well be proud of her sons. We fathers miss our sons, but we thrill with pride, aye, and joy, when we remember the cause for which our boys died. The mothers of England—what can we say of them? No noble Roman matrons ever sent forth their sons with greater willingness than did the wives and sweethearts of England send their men-folk. Fathers, mothers, sisters, and others, all gave their quota, and gave enthusiastically.

The men who have fought, whose names are recorded here, and who have survived the terrible struggle, have our intense and unstinted gratitude. The men whose photographs are here reproduced, these we cannot thank, we cannot express what we feel; but need we try?

After all, they have died as they lived; men who played the game, aye, played to the final whistle. They have left us a noble example; may we not pray that our Father will enable us all to follow in their steps, to play the game and do our duty to our God and to our fellow-man.

"The echo of 'their' deeds is ringing yet,
Will ring for aye. All else . . . . .
                Let us forget."

RICHARD HUGGARD

S. John's Vicarage, Barnsley
   October 27th 1919

By R. F. OAKES
Hon. Secretary Yorkshire Rugby Union

"This Light and Darkness in our chaos join'd,
What shall divide? The God within the mind."

THE Yorkshire Rugby Union are proud—yes, mightily proud—of the glorious part their players have played in this ghastly world war which has just been so bitterly and doggedly fought—and so handsomely won.

To-day, every schoolboy must have read, and read, I am sure, with a great glow of pride, of that wonderful headlong rush the Rugby men made when the call to arms was sounded—when every "Rugger" club in the British Isles immediately closed its doors to its beloved Rugger—"Rugger" for which, year after year, sacrifices had been cheerfully made in order to keep the flag flying and the great and glorious game going, healthy and strong.

We all now know of their great deeds of "derring do" on that greater field—their indomitable courage, their healthy cheerfulness under the most exacting, trying, and awful conditions that man has ever been called upon to face and to endure. We now know how splendidly the Rugby footballer, in common with every British soldier, fought—aye, and how magnificently he died!

All this is, to-day, glorious history—history unparalleled in the whole annals of the world—history which will never be surpassed—history which will become an intense part of every British boy's education. Yes—and history which will be cherished and held sacred by every Rugby lover for all time.

And the Yorkshire Rugby Union man played his part, truly, faithfully, and well in this ghastly tragedy.

Should there be a single lurking doubt, reader, in your mind, turn over these pages. Read the report of the last General Meeting of the Yorkshire Rugby Union. Look over those lists—wonderful lists—of the men who joined H.M. Forces—volunteers all. Read over that list of "Honours Won." Yes, and read over and ponder deeply, that greater list of "Our Glorious Dead."

Every list breathes honour and duty.

Read, too, that letter from Colonel Davison—a man who knew—what he says about a Yorkshireman, and a Rugby footballer!

Yorkshiremen!! Be proud of your sons—and you women of Yorkshire, be proud that you bore such sons, for nobler sons never breathed.

To-day, Yorkshire is all the poorer by these terrible losses—aye, but all the richer for the glorious example they have set us, by their wonderful courage and devotion.

Elsewhere in these pages a reverent tribute is paid to the memory of these truly noble boys—white men all.

But there was another magnificent side to the lives of these wonderful boys, which, except perhaps to their own intimates, hardly ever saw the gleaming light of publicity—their everyday life.

It is to this side I would now wish to refer, and in so doing endeavour, in simple language, to pay my humble and heartfelt tribute to their memory—a memory of which, thank God, nothing can ever rob us.

I cannot claim to be a Yorkshireman—not, indeed, that I would ever wish to, for that little County of Durham is as dear to me as I know Yorkshire is to a Yorkshireman. But it has been my great privilege, for some years now, to occupy the position of Hon. Secretary to the Yorkshire Rugby Union, and by virtue of that office I have been brought into constant contact, into close and intimate relationship, with these very boys whose photographs appear in these pages—many were my close personal friends.

So I claim to know, not from a superficial knowledge, but from actual experience, something of these boys—that " something " which, I timidly venture to say, was perhaps not known, or more probably imperfectly understood, even by their parents themselves. That " something " which comes to light, gradually at first, and then slowly develops as the restraining and refining influences of home life partially cease— when the boy becomes the man. Yes, that " something " which is at once a terrible fear and a fervent hope—the fear which catches at the heart strings of every mother—the hope which she has silently built up within her from the moment her boy first saw the light of day, when she realises that this great big world, with all its joys and sorrows, its great hopes and bitter disappointments, its enormous temptations so easy to succumb to, so terribly difficult to evade, are opening out to her boy.

We, of the Yorkshire Rugby Union, see these boys at what is undoubtedly the most critical period of their lives. It is with this knowledge of these boys that I say, and say truthfully and without fear of contradiction, that cleaner, nobler, more wholesome boys never lived. We have seen them on the field when play has been keen and exciting—they were clean. We have seen them off the field, in their cooler, collected moments—they were straight. Clean on the footer field, they carried that cleanliness of the sporting instinct into their everyday life until it became cleanliness of soul.

They have left to the younger generation—aye, to posterity for all time—a shining example of heroism, duty, and sacrifice unequalled and unsurpassed.

When I look back over the vista of those last five agonising years, there comes to me that indescribable twinging of the heart when I think I shall never see these boys again—for somehow one grew to love them with a greater love than one ever thought possible. Their kindness, their courtesy, their joyous enthusiasm for the game, their eager desire to lighten one's work, their splendid sense of fairness and sportsmanship, and, above and beyond all, their wholesome cleanliness of everyday life, was such that they endeared themselves to everybody with whom they came into contact. To know them was an education—an education in its highest sense. To get amongst them made one feel cleaner and better.

In all this one finds all the elements that go to make the man—and men they were.

These boys have left a glorious and imperishable memory to Rugby footballers.

That is why I say the Yorkshire Rugby Union are proud of those players of theirs who have crossed the line for the last time, in the greatest game of their lives.

We will for ever cherish their memory.

Well may the mothers of these boys be proud of their sons. They can truly lift up their bowed heads, and through those anguished tears—tears the cost of which only a mother knows—be proud indeed that they bore such sons—sons who died as they lived—clean, straight, wholesome, and true.

R. F. OAKES.

JOHN ABBOTT KING

Lance-Corporal 1/10th Liverpool Scottish
Missing 9th August 1916
Headingley, Yorkshire, and English International Forward

BY R. F. OAKES

" WELL played, King ; played, indeed, Sir."

How those critical but delightful Twickenham crowds cheered the great little man ! And how the breasts of that little, but enthusiastic crowd of " Headingley " and Yorkshire supporters used to swell with a mighty—and a perfectly justifiable—pride, at the great doings of their idolised " Jack " King !

But I wonder how many of those great International crowds of Twickenham, Inverleith, Lansdowne Road, Cardiff, Newport, and Swansea, who were both so astounded and so delighted at the unflinching pluck and great play of this boy, had even the remotest conception of the true greatness of this player ? I don't mean their knowledge of his prowess as a player, but of the greatness of a soulful man. *Mens sana in corpore sano* was never more fitly applied to any man than to Jack King.

The 4th August, 1914, is too indelibly inscribed on the tablets of every Briton's memory to be more than casually mentioned here. At that time, and for a few weeks prior to this never-to-be-forgotten day, Jack King had staying with him at his farm at Ben Rhydding one of his " Headingley " footer friends, T. D. Lumb—a rare good forward, who, like a great many of the " Headingley " players, has made the supreme sacrifice. " Busty " Lumb and Jack were busy haymaking, when the former's mobilisation papers were handed to him, Lumb being already an enthusiastic Territorial in the Yorkshire Hussars of some years standing.

" Sorry, Jack," said Lumb, " but I'll have to chuck now, pack up, and make a bee line for headquarters—we are called up."

Before leaving, Jack had just time to make a few inquiries from his friend Lumb, as to the mode of procedure *re* joining the Yorkshire Hussars, " For," added Jack, " I intend to come with you."

Without fuss, or show, or noise, and with a few instructions to his sisters as to the management of the farm, Jack King left his home on the morning of Thursday, 6th August, 1914, for the headquarters of the Yorkshire Hussars. Never for one moment dreaming, in face of the imperative call of King and Country, that he would have anything but a clean walk straight into this famous Yorkshire Regiment, Jack got his first shock that day. "Sorry, King," said the Recruiting Officer, when Jack presented himself, "but I'm afraid we cannot take you." "For why"? inquired King. "Because," answered the R.O., "the Army Regulations state the minimum height to be 5 feet 6 inches ; you are only 5 feet 5." Jack had reckoned without a thorough knowledge of the King's Regulations!!

For a moment he was completely nonplussed and upset, but quickly recovering himself, he threw out that 45-inch chest of his and said, "Well, I've come purposely through here to join the same regiment as my friend Lumb, and I'm simply going to stick here until you do take me in."

Whether or not Jack managed to grow that extra inch in the three days he waited, is not officially stated, but the military records show that Jack King became a Trooper in His Britannic Majesty's Army on 9th August, 1914.

That is just one little side light of a great many similar instances of love and duty in the life of this famous International.

Here is another, equally true, which I can personally testify to, and one which casts even a greater halo round the memory of this noble-hearted boy. The Yorkshire Hussars, in common with the greater part of the cavalry in France, at this particular period, were chiefly engaged in patrol and police duty. This by no means appealed to the big heart and active mind of Jack, and after a few months of this work he became very restive, as his frequent letters to me clearly showed, and he began to chafe and fret "to be more of a soldier" as he put it, and must needs try and get transferred to an infantry regiment. Meeting, one day while in France, a lot of old Rugby friends, who were members of the 1/10th Liverpool Scottish Regiment—amongst whom was the famous old English forward Slocock, then a captain in the Liverpool Scottish—nothing would satisfy Jack but that he must, somehow or other, join them. Application for his transfer was immediately made; in due course his papers came through, and from that time until the fateful 9th August, 1916, he was known in the Army as Lance-Corporal J. A. King, " X " Company, 1/10th Liverpool Scottish.

Yes—of his own free will, he preferred to share the hard lot of the infantryman in those horrifying, waterlogged, knee-deep mud trenches, to the comparatively easier lot and safety of police duty behind the lines.

But that was just Jack King. His sense of duty was always such, that he steadfastly refused to allow any other considerations to influence him.

August 9th, 1916, was a sad day for the 1/10th Liverpool Scottish. Three times that day did they attempt to take Guillemont, and three times were they repulsed, the flower of this grand regiment going down before the hellish machine gun fire of the Boche. It is a date sacred to every living member of the " Headingley " Club.

Jack King's career as a soldier—just a simple soldier (he refused to listen to any suggestion that he should take up a commission)—was marked by those same traits which had endeared him to all his football friends—brimful of mirth, kind, loving, generous, and absolutely unselfish, ever keen and anxious to do his very utmost in whatever he took in hand, living to do what he died for—duty, nobly done!

Perhaps if these lines meet the eye of Colonel Davidson, of the 1/10th Liverpool Scottish, he will forgive the liberty I take of quoting a part of an exceedingly kind and sympathetic letter he was good enough to write the Misses King at the time Jack was reported missing—

> It is hardly necessary for me to testify to his conduct at such a time—anyone who knew your brother would know that he could always be relied upon to play the man.
>
> When I saw him, absolutely cool and collected under a murderous machine gun fire, with shells falling all round, one thanked God for such men to set such a priceless example. He was absolutely lionhearted, and had he come through, I should have promoted him on the field and recommended him for D.C.M.
>
> It was a sad day for football. We can ill spare men like these, but if another game of football is never played in Britain, the game has done well, for after two years' command in the field, I am convinced that the *Rugby footballer makes the finest soldier in the world*.

What a noble tribute to a noble boy! And can a greater tribute be paid to this fine, manly game, than that paid to it by this very boy, in a letter written to the writer of this short appreciation, just before going "over the top" for the last time—a letter which I deeply treasure—

> I am absolutely A1 in every way—but one can never tell, and so long as I don't disgrace the old Rugby game, I don't think I mind.

Jack King disgrace the Rugby game! No, a thousand times, No!

A few others may, perhaps, have ascended to higher heights on the football field, but none certainly have ever out-shone Jack King in his love for this—the greatest of all games—our beloved Rugger.

Perhaps Jack King's greatest charm was his modesty in all things—not that he was insensible to the wonderful homage paid to him by his many friends and admirers—far from it, for he had a deep sense of appreciation.

But it is equally certain that he never looked for acknowledgement—never imagined himself, or wished others to imagine, that he had done anything more meritorious either on a football field, or when he gave his life for his Country, than the veriest third teamer, or the rawest recruit.

And to-day! Not a cheer! Not a flower or a cross to mark the sacred spot where this hero fell! Jack King would not have it otherwise. But his memory is enshrined in the hearts of all his "Headingley" and Yorkshire friends. The glorious part he has played is the manifestation of Britain's soul. He has joined that noble band which has helped to save the world. He now knows the reason of it all.

Yes, truly, "Well played, King; played, indeed, Sir."

> So, you'll live, you'll live, young fellow my lad,
> In the gleam of the evening star,
> In the wood note wild,
> In the laugh of the child,
> In all sweet things that are.
> And you'll never die, my wonderful boy,
> While life is noble and true,
> For all our beauty, and hope, and joy,
> We will owe to our lads like you.

R. F. OAKES.

THE following photographs bear silent but eloquent testimony to the service our men gave, and the sacrifices they made, for King and Country

It is regretted that the Secretaries of Leeds University Leeds Training College, Sedbergh School, West Riding Regiment, and York St. John's College have been unable to furnish the records of those of their members who joined H.M. forces.

If I should die, think only this of me:
  That there's some corner of a foreign field
That is for ever England. There shall be
  In that rich earth a richer dust concealed;
A dust whom England bore, shaped, made aware,
  Gave, once, her flowers to love, her ways to roam,
A body of England's, breathing English air,
  Washed by the rivers, blest by suns of home.

And think, this heart, all evil shed away,
  A pulse in the eternal mind, no less
Gives somewhere back the thoughts by England given;
  Her sights and sounds; dreams happy as her day
And laughter, learnt of friends; and gentleness,
  In hearts at peace, under an English heaven.

—RUPERT BROOKE

AMPLEFORTH COLLEGE

Members who Joined the Forces

AINSCOUGH, M. J.
BARNEWALL, Lt. Hon. R. N. F.
BARTON, Lt. O. J.
BEACH, G.
CALDWELL, Lt. J. B.
CHAMBERLAIN, Lt. N.
CHAMBERLAIN, Lt. W. G.
CRAVOS, F. S.
CRAVOS, Sec.-Lt. C.
DE GUINGAND, Cadet F.
EMERY, Lt. H. J.
EMERY, Sec.-Lt. R. G.
ENCOMBE, Sec.-Lt. Viscount
FARRELL, Lt. G. E.
FOLEY, J.
GERRARD, Sec.-Lt. J. M. H.
HALL, Lt. G. F. M.
HARTE-BARRY, Sec.-Lt. G.
HODGE, Cadet W.
KELLY, Lt. A. P.
KELLY, Sec.-Lt. J. O.
KNOWLES, Lt. V.
KNOWLES, Sec.-Lt. C. J.
LANCASTER, Lt. S.
LE FEVRE, Sec.-Lt. E.
LISTON, R. P.
LISTON, C. P.
LISTON, Capt. W. P.
LONG, Sec.-Lt. F. W.
LYNCH, Sec.-Lt. R.
MACPHERSON, Sec.-Lt. C. F.
MARTIN, Lt. E. J.
MARTIN, Sec.-Lt. H. A.
MASSEY, Cadet E. J.
McDONALD, Capt. A. J.
McDONALD, Sec.-Lt. D. P.
McDONALD, —.
McGHEE, Sec.-Lt. T.
MORROGH-BERNARD, Lt. F. J.
MORROGH-BERNARD, Lt. J. E.
MORICE. Lt. J. F.
NAREY, Sec.-Lt. V. G.
POWER, Lt. R. J.
ROCHFORD, Capt. L. H.
ROCHFORD, Lt. S. A.
ROCHFORD, Sec.-Lt. W.
SCOTT, Hon. M.
SIMPSON, Sec.-Lt. C. R.
SIMPSON, Cadet J. G.
UNSWORTH, Surgeon L.
WELSH, Lt. T. V.
WILLIAMS, Lt. L. T.
WRIGHT, Capt. A. F. M.

The Fallen

BARNEWALL, Lt. Hon. R. N. F.
CRAVOS, Sec.-Lt. C.
GERRARD, Sec.-Lt. J. M. H.
HALL, Lt. G. F. M.
LISTON, Capt. W. P.
LONG, Sec.-Lt. F. W.
MARTIN, Lt. E. J.
McDONALD, Capt. A. J.
McGHEE, Sec.-Lt. T.
MORROGH-BERNARD, Lt. F. A.
NAREY, Sec.-Lt. V. G.
POWER, Lt. R. J.
WILLIAMS, Lt. L.

Honours

KELLY, Lt. A. P., M.C.
ROCHFORD, Capt. L. H., D.S.C. and bar, D.F.C.

GERRARD, J. MAURICE H.
2nd Lieutenant Royal Field Artillery
Killed August 28th 1918
Ampleforth College R.F.C.

HALL, GEORGE F. M.
Lieutenant Royal Berkshire Regiment
Killed September 28th 1915
Ampleforth College

LISTON, W. P. ST. L.
Captain Leinster Regiment
Killed April 12th 1917
Ampleforth College

MARTIN, E J.
Lieutenant Royal Warwickshire Regiment
Killed July 1st 1916
Ampleforth College

McGHEE, T. A.
2nd Lieutenant Argyll and Sutherland Highlanders
Killed September 20th 1918
Ampleforth College

POWER, R. J.
Lieutenant 33rd Punjabis
Killed in action in German East Africa July 19th 1917
Ampleforth College

WILLIAMS, L.
Lieutenant South Wales Borderers
Killed September 11th 1915
Ampleforth College

BAILDON

Members Who Joined the Forces

BARKER, Dvr. G., R.F.A.
BUCKINGHAM, P.
CONSTANTINE, Capt. R., Cyc. C.
DENBY, Gnr. H., H.A.C.
ELLIOTT, A.
ELLISON, Sgt. W., 1/6 West Yorks.
EMMISON, Lt. P.C.B., 1/6 West Yks.
FAIRLESS, Pte. A., Can. Force
FIELD, Sec.-Lt. H. W., Cyc. C.
HILL, J. R.
HOLMES, Sgt. W., R.G.A.
HOLMES, Cpl. W. W., A.P.C.
JUKES, Lt. H., R.F.A.
KEIGHLEY, Pte. P., 1/6 West Yks.
LAW, Sec.-Lt. H. M. B., R.F.C.
LUND, Lt. C., Indian Army
LUND, Lt. T., Nrth. Fus.
MANN, Bd. J., R.F.A.
MARGETTS, Pte. J. T. C., 1/6 W.Y.
MELHUISH, Capt. H., Indian Army
METCALFE, Pte. J., Scottish Fus.
MOORHOUSE, Sgt.-In. H. P., 25 R.F.
ODDY, Lt. R., West Yorks.
POLLARD, Pte. W., 15 West Yorks.
ROBINSON, Dvr. A., A.S.C. (M.T.)
ROBINSON, Lt. O., West Riding
SHIPP, Lt. C. L., R.F.A.
SIDEBOTHAM, Capt. Rev. A. E., Army Chaplain
STEVENSON, Cpl. J. L., A.S.C. (M.T.)
TATTERSALL, H.
WHITE, Dvr. G., R.F.A.
WHITTAKER, Capt. F. W., 1/6 W.Y.
WHITTAKER, Sec.-Lt. J., W. Riding
WORSNOP, Pte. T., 1/6 West Yorks.

The Fallen

CONSTANTINE, Capt. R., Cyc. C.
FIELD, Sec.-Lt. H. W., Cyc. C.
KEIGHLEY, Pte. P., 1/6 West Yk.
LAW, Sec.-Lt. H. M. B., R.F.C.
LUND, Lt. T., Nrth. Fus.
MARGETTS, Pte. J. T. C. 1/6 W.Y.
WHITTAKER, Sec.-Lt. J., W. Riding

Honours

ELLISON, Sgt. W., D.C.M.
WHITTAKER, Capt. F. W., M.C., twice mentioned in despatches

CONSTANTINE, ROBERT BAXANDALL
Captain 2/6th West Yorkshire Regiment (attached "L" Corps Cyclist Battalion)
Killed 1919
Baildon R.F.C.

FIELD, HAROLD W.
2nd Lieutenant Cyclists' Corps
Killed May 1918
Baildon R.F.C

KEIGHLEY, PHILIP
Private 1/6th West Yorkshire Regiment
Killed December 26th 1915
Baildon R.F.C.

MARGETTS, J. T. C.
Private 1/6 West Yorkshire Regiment
Killed December 10th 1915
Baildon R.F.C.

BARNSLEY

Members who Joined the Forces

Asquith, Capt. G., M.G.C.
Beck, Pte. G. E.
Beeken, Cpl. J., East Yorks.
Bentley, C.Q.M.S. J. G., Y. & L.
Bentley, Sgt. J., M.G.C.
Braham, Cpl. W., Y. & L.
Brooke, A.
Brown, Capt. S. E. V., N.Z. Force
Carr, Major A. G. H., R.A.F.
Cassells, Capt. G., R.E.
Clegg, Capt. C. H., Y. & L.
Crossfield, Sgt. H., West Yorks.
Davies, Sgt. R., Y. & L.
Dixon, Lt. W. J., Y. & L.
Fox, Sgt. P., Y. & L.
Gray, Lt. G. D.
Griffiths, Pte. Ivor Linc. Regt.
Hall, Fl.-Lt. E. D, R.A.F.
Harrison, Sgt. G., Y. & L.
Hewitt, Capt. G. G., Y & L.
Holmes, Gnr. G., R.F.A.
Howell, Capt. Dr. T., R.A.M.C.
Hudson, Capt. G. H., Y. & L.
Huggard, Capt. L. D. R., Y. & L.
Huggard, Capt. Rev. R., Y. & L.
Huggard, Lt. Hewitt, East Yks.
Hutchinson, Lt. H., West Yorks.
Hyslop, Pte. J. G., Cameron H.
Jardine, Capt. Dr. W. C., R.A.M.C
Jones, Sgt. A., Y. & L.
Kell, Lt. W., Y. & L.
Knowles, Capt. H., R.A.M.C.
Legard, Gnr. H. R., R.F.A.
Lowrance, A., Red Cross M.A.
Loy, Cpl. H., D.L.I.
MacPhail, Capt. E. J., R.S. Fus.
Mindham, Lt. F. W., Nigeria Regt.
Nelson, Capt. E. A., R.E.
Nicholson, Lt. E. C., East Yorks.
Nicholson, Cpl. S., K.R.R.
Northern, T.
Raley, Capt. W. H. G., Yks. Regt.
Raley, Lt. Walter H., Y. & L.
Raley, Capt. S. C., D.L.I.
Raynor, Pte. E., Aust. Forces
Richardson, Pte. O. G., West Y.
Spedding, Sgt. G. H., K.O.Y.L.I.
Stuart, Mechanic G. A. L., R.A.F.
Sutch, Lt. R. H., R.F.A.
Sykes, Pte. S., Y. & L.
Symonds, Sap. A., R E.
Tibbetts, Ft.-Lt. J. L., R.A.F.
Todd, Lt. F. W., R.A.F.
Townend, Capt. H., Y. & L.
Umbers, Lt. E. H., R.A.F.
Ward, Sgt. F., Y. & L.

The Fallen

Beck, Pte. G. E.
Brooke, A.
Gray, Lt. G. D.
Harrison, Sgt. G., Y. & L.
Hewitt, Capt. G. G., Y. & L.
Huggard, Capt. L. D. R., Y. & L.
Huggard, Lt. Hewitt, East Yks.
Knowles, Capt. H., R.A.M.C.
Nicholson, Cpl. S., K.R.R.
Raley, Capt. W. H. G., Yorks. Rg.
Raley, Lt. Walter H.
Raynor, Pte. E., Australian Force

Honours

Carr, Major A. G. H., O.B.E. (Military)
Cassells, Capt. G., M.C.
Howell, Capt. T., M.C.
Huggard, Capt. R., M.A., M.B.E. (Military)
Jones, Sgt. A., M.M.
Knowles, Capt., M.C.
Nicholson, Lt. E. C., M.C.

BECK, GEORGE EDWARD
Private 13th York and Lancaster Regiment
Killed on the Somme June 18th 1916
Barnsley R.F.C.

GRAY, GEORGE DONALD
Lieutenant 14th York and Lancaster Regiment
Killed at Ervillers May 5th 1917
Barnsley R.F.C.

HEWITT, GEORGE ALFRED GUEST
Captain 1/5th York and Lancaster Regiment
Killed at Bourlon Village November 27th 1917
Barnsley R.F.C.

HUGGARD, LEWIS DUDLEY RICHARD
Captain 13th York and Lancaster Regiment
Killed in France June 26th 1917
Barnsley R F.C

HUGGARD, HEWITT
Lieutenant 6th East Yorkshire Regiment
Killed at Suvla Bay August 9th 1915
Barnsley R.F.C.

KNOWLES, H. R., M.C.
Captain Royal Army Medical Corps
Killed on the Somme July 1916
Barnsley R.F.C.

NICHOLSON, S.
Corporal King's Royal Rifles
Killed in action on the Somme
Barnsley R.F.C.

RALEY, WALTER HUGH
2nd Lieutenant 5th York and Lancaster Regiment
Killed at Fleurbaix May 14th 1915
Barnsley R.F.C.

RALEY, WILLIAM HENRY GEORGE
Captain 3rd Alexandra Princess of Wales' Own Yorkshire Regiment
Killed at Givenchy June 15th 1915
Barnsley R.F.C.

BATLEY

Members who Joined the Forces

Aspinwall, C.
Auty, J. S.
Beattie, C. S.
Beattie, T. M.
Blamires, B.
Craik, T. E.
Critchley, L. C.
Ellis, G. R.
Hirst, C.
Hodgson, C. E.
Ineson, D. G.
Jubb, C.
Jubb, F.
Jubb, G. B.
Kaye, F. G.
Kemp, M.
Morris, A.
Parker, G.
Parker, P. C.
Pritchard, M.
Senior, G. T.
Senior, J. T.
Senior, W. T.
Shaw, A.
Shaw, L.
Sheard, B.
Sheard, G.
Simpson, B. W.
Simpson, R.
Smith, D. C.
Stubley, C. T.
Sykes, F.
Sykes, G.
Talbot, J. H.
Talbot, J. W.
Talbot, R. K.
Thornton, W. C.
Thresh, J. B. T.
Walker, H. G.
Ward, C.
Ward, F. J.
Watson, D. C.
Watson, G. W.
Williamson, R.

The Fallen

Ellis, Sgt. G. R.
Senior, Lt. J. T.
Senior, Lt. W. T.
Simpson, Lt. R.
Smith, Capt. D. C.
Sykes, Sgt. G.
Watson, Pte. D. C.
Walker, Lt. H. G.

Honours

Craik, Major T. E., M.C., M.G.C.
Hirst, Lt. C., M.C., K.O.Y.L.I.
Parker, Major P. C., M.C., W.Y.
Shaw, Capt. L., M.C.

ELLIS, GEORGE RONALD
Lieutenant Royal Flying Corps
Killed July 26th 1917
Batley R.F.C.

SENIOR, J.
Lieutenant Royal Flying Corps
Killed May 9th 1918
Batley R.F.C.

SENIOR, WALTER TALBOT
Lieutenant 2/6th West Yorkshire Regiment
Missing at Thiepval September 3rd 1916
Batley R.F.C.

SIMPSON, R. H.
Lieutenant 4th Lancashire Fusiliers attached 2nd Lancashire Fusiliers
Killed July 9th 1915
Batley R.F.C.

SMITH, D. C.
Captain 16th West Yorkshire Regiment
Missing July 1st 1916
Batley R.F.C.

SYKES, G.
Sergeant 1/4th King's Own Yorkshire Light Infantry
Died of wounds April 1918
Batley R.F.C.

WATSON, DONALD JAMES
Private Liverpool Scottish, King's Liverpool Regiment
Killed January 3rd 1918
Batley R.F.C.

HORTON now BRADFORD

Members who Joined the Forces

ACKROYD, Lt. F., A.S.C., M.T.
APPLEYARD, Capt. J. E., 8 W.Y.
BELDON, Lt. E., 6 West Yorks.
BLOOMER, Pte. A. K., 1/6 West Y.
BONSOR, R., Prince Albert's Horse (South Africa)
BROCKLEBANK, J. W. F., Yorks. D.
BROCKLEBANK, H. L., Yorks. D.
BROCKLEHURST, Pte. F., 1/6 W.Y.
BROUGH, R.S.M. A., 2/6 West Yks.
CORDINGLEY, Cpl. L., 1/6 West Yk.
CORDINGLEY, Lt. R. C., Can. Inf.
CRYER, Pte. H. S., 1/6 West Yorks.
CUTCLIFFE, Pte. H. J., West Yorks.
FIELDING, L.-Cpl. A., M.G.C.
FLAXINGTON, Lt. W., West Rdg. R.
FOSTER, Lt. L., West Riding Rgt.
FOX, Pte. M., R.A.M.C. (T.)
GARBUTT, Lt. D. G., 6 West Yorks.
GARBUTT, L.-Cpl. W., 6 West Yorks.
GOODALL, Lt. F., 6 West Yorks.
GREENOUGH, Pte. H. S., West Yks.
HALEY, Capt. J. A., R.E.
HELLEWELL, Capt. D., West Yorks.
HINDLEY, Capt. J., 17 K.R.R.
HOLDSWORTH, Gnr. E., R.G.A.
HOLDSWORTH, Lt. J., R.A.F.
HOLT, Lt. W. P., R.F.A.
HOWLETT, L.-Cpl. T. E., 1/6 W.Y.
HOWSON, Lt. J. F., R.G.A.
HUMPHRIES, Pte. J. B., R.A.M.C.
HUMPHRIES, Lt. W., West Yorks.
JOWETT, Lt. H. A., 6 West Yorks.
LONGFIELD, D., Despatch Rider, R.E. (Signals)
MARCHANT, B. W., R.E. Special Co.
MITCHELL, Sgt. R., R.E.
MITTON, Capt., N. V., R.A.M C.
MOSLEY, Cpl. A., West Yorks.
NAREY, Lt. B. P., 1/6 West Yorks.
NAREY, Lt. V. G., West Riding Rg.
ODDY, Lt. J. R. R., R.E.
OWTHWAITE, Sgt. R. M., 1 Can. Tk.
PARSEY, Lt. R., 1/6 West Yorks.
PETTY, Lt. R. L., 3 West Yorks.
POLLARD, Capt. J., K.O.Y.L.I.
ROBINSON, Capt. F. V., West Yorks
ROBINSON, Staff-Capt. E., Ind. Ay.
SELLERS, Sgt. S., 1/6 West Yorks.
SIMPSON, A., Yorks. Dragoons
SMITH, Lt. R., R.E.
SMITH, Pte. F., Coldstream Guards
THOMPSON, Lt. T., 1/6 West Yorks.
TOWNSON, Lt. H., R.F.C.
VICKERMANN, Sgt. F., 1/6 West Yk.
WADE, Lt. J. A., 6 West Yorks.
WALMSLEY, C.S.M. W., 1/6 W.Y.
WHITE, Capt. F., K.O.Y.L.I.
WILSON, Lt. E., 18 West Yorks.
WOOD, Lt. H. E., West Riding Rg.
WOODHEAD, Lt. W., R.E.
WRAY, Lt. S. H., Labour Corps

The Fallen

APPLEYARD, Capt. J. E., 8 W.Y.
BLOOMER, Pte. A. K., 1/6 West Y.
BROUGH, R.S.M. A., 2/6 West Yks.
CORDINGLEY, Lt. R. C., Can. Inf.
CRYER, Pte. H. S., 1/6 West Yorks.
HOWLETT, L.-Cpl. T. E., 1/6 W.Y.
HUMPHRIES, Lt. W., West Yorks.
MITCHELL, Sgt. R., R.E.
MOSLEY, Cpl. A., West Yorks.
NAREY, Lt. V. G., West Riding Rg.
PETTY, Lt. R. L., 3 West Yorks.
ROBINSON, Capt. F. V., West Yorks
SMITH, Lt. R., R.E.
TOWNSON, Lt. H., R.F.C.
WALMSLEY, C.S.M. W., 1/6 W.Y.
WHITE, Capt. F., K.O.Y.L.I.

Honours

APPLEYARD, Capt. J. E., 8 West Yorks., M.C.
HALEY, Capt. J. A., R.E., M.C.
HOLT, Lt. W. P., R.F.A., M.C.
MITCHELL, Sgt. R., R.E., M.M.
WALMSLEY, C.S.M. W., 1/6 West Yorks., Croix-de-Guerre
WHITE, Capt. F., K.O.Y.L.I., M.C.
BROUGH, C.S.M. A., 2/6 West Yorks., M.C., D.C.M.

AIREY, H. W. S.
2nd Lieutenant 1/5th West Yorkshire Regiment
Killed in action January 11th 1917
Horton R.F.C.

APPLEYARD, J. E., M.C.
Captain 8th West Yorkshire Regiment
Killed in action July 20th 1918
Horton R.F.C. and Bradford R.F.C.

CORDINGLEY, ROBERT CECIL
Lieutenant 9th Canadian Brigade Machine Gun Corps
Killed in action in France June 4th 1916
Bradford R.F.C.

CRYER, H. S.
Private 1/6th West Yorkshire Regiment
Killed in action August 19th 1915
Bradford R.F.C.

HOWLETT, T.
Corporal 1/6th West Yorkshire Regiment
Killed in action July 1915
Bradford R.F.C.

HUMPHRIES, W. R.
2nd Lieutenant 18th West Yorkshire Regiment
Killed in action July 28th 1916
Bradford R.F.C.

MITCHELL, REUBEN, M.M.
Sergeant No. 2 Special Company Royal Engineers
Killed in action April 6th 1917
Bradford R.F.C.

MOSLEY, W. A.
Corporal 16th West Yorkshire Regiment
Killed in action July 1st 1916
Bradford R.F.C.

NAREY, V. G.
Lieutenant 11th attached to 8th Duke of Wellington's Regiment
Died of wounds received in action October 15th 1916
Horton R.F.C. and Bradford R.F.C.

PETTY, R. L.
Lieutenant 3rd West Yorkshire Regiment, attached to 7th North Staffs.
Killed in action at Berker August 31st 1918
Bradford R.F.C.

ROBINSON, F. V.
Lieutenant West Yorkshire Regiment (2nd Bradford Pals)
Killed May 3rd 1917
Bradford R.F.C.

SMITH, C. R.
Lieutenant M Company Special Brigade Royal Engineers
Killed in action June 11th 1917
Bradford R.F.C.

TOWNSON, H.
2nd Lieutenant 3rd West Yorkshire Regiment attached Royal Air Force
Killed night of April 20th 1917
Bradford R.F.C.

WALMSLEY, W., Croix-de-Guerre
Company-Sergeant-Major 1/6th West Yorkshire Regiment
Taken prisoner April 1917. Died of influenza in Germany after the armistice
Bradford R.F.C.

WHITE, F. H., M.C.
Captain 12th King's Own Yorkshire Light Infantry
Died of wounds April 16th 1918
Horton R.F.C. and Bradford R.F.C.

BRADFORD GRAMMAR SCHOOL

Members who Joined the Forces

ACKROYD, H.
AMBLER, G.
ATKINSON, J.
BANKS, Sec.-Lt. A T., Indian Army
BEDFORD, T. H. B.
BENNETT, WLFD.
BRAYSHAW Lt. O. B., R.A.F.
BUCKLEY, A.
BUSFIELD, A. H.
CLARKSON, G.
DAVIES, A. E. C.
FISHER, Lt. J. H., West Yorks.
FLEMING, Lt. O. D., R.G.A.
GLOYNE, Cdt. R. W. D., R.M.C. Quetta
GRATTAN, H.
GRIEVE, Lt. J. W., R.G.A.
HARLAND, G. E.
HART, Lt. R., West Yorks.
HICK, Sec.-Lt. B., West Yorks.
HOLDSWORTH, Cdt. R. F., O.C.B.
HOLLIDAY, Ft.-Cdt. C. H., R.A.F.
HOLMES, Sec.-Lt. I., West Yorks.
HUBY, H.
INGHAM, J. B.
KNIGHT, S. H.
LEACH, Sec.-Lt. F., R.G.A.
LING, Lt. W. H. G., R.A.F.
LOSEBY, H. V.
LUND, Sec.-Lt. C., Ghurka Regt.
LUND, Cdt. F. K., O.C.B.
McKECHNIE, W.O. C. A., M.F.A.

MELLOR, Lt. N. E., R.A.F.
MIDDLEBROOK, Lt. S. M., R.G.A.
MOELLER, W.O. D., R.N.V.R.
MOFFAT, Sec.-Lt. J. F., Seaforth H.
MOSS, Sec.-Lt. W. T. G., R.F.C.
NEWBY, Pte. C. A., West Yorks.
NEWHILL, Sec.-Lt. J., R.A.F.
PEATFIELD, Pte. E. C., Artist's Rfl.
PRATT, Ft.-Cdt. A. S. R., R.A.F.
PRATT, Sec.-Lt. B. J. A., West Yks.
PRIESTLEY, L.-Cpl. D. W., D.L.I.
PRIESTLEY, Lt. L. S., R.G.A.
RHODES, Lt. F. A., R.A.F.
ROBINSON, Lt. E. C., Gharwal Rfls.
ROTHERAY, A.M. R. E., R.A.F
SANDS, Sec.-Lt. S. E., R.G.A.
SCOTT, W.O. G., Aux. Csr. R.N.T.
SHAW, Pte. F. C., R.A.F.
SHEER, Lt. P. S., R.G.A.
SMART, Cdt. G. F., O.C.B.
SMITH, Sec.-Lt. N. H., West Yorks.
SPEIGHT, Capt. J. L., West Yorks.
STANCOMBE, Pte. B. M., West Yks.
STAYNES, Sec.-Lt. T. A., West Yks.
SYMONS, Srg. Prob. J. S., R.N.V.R.
WARD, Cdt. F. H., O.C.B.
WATSON, Sec.-Lt. C. F. K., R.G.A.
WATSON, Lt. D , R.G.A.
WATSON, Sec.-Lt. W. V. C., W.Y.
WAUGH, A.B. F.
WILKINSON, Sec.-Lt. A., R.A.F.
WOODCOCK, Lt. T. A., P. of W.'s

The Fallen

BARKER, Capt. G., West Yorks.
BEDFORD, Sec.-Lt. A. W., W. Yks.
BILLING, Sec.-Lt. J., K.O.Y.L.I.
BOWER, Lt. E. H., York & Lancs.
COWGILL, Sec.-Lt. W. A. F., R.F.A.
GRATTAN, Pte. H., Worcester Rgt.
HANBY, Sec.-Lt. F. J., R. Sussex
MELLOR, Lt. N. E., R.A.F.
MOSS, Sec.-Lt. W. T. G., R.F.C.
PEEL, Lt. A., Royal Bucks. Regt
PRITCHARD, Sec.-Lt. D., R.W.F.
RHODES, Gnr. C., R.F.A.

RIGG, Sig. H. S. R., R.N.V.R.
ROOME, Pte. J. M., Leicester Regt.
RUSHWORTH, Rfm. F., K.R.R.
SLICER, Lt. P. S., R.G.A.
SMITH, Sec.-Lt. N. H., West Yorks.
SUGDEN, B. R., King's Liverpool
SUNDERLAND, Pte. D. S., Nth. Fus.
THOMPSON, Lt. W. D., R.W.F.
WHITEHEAD, Sec.-Lt. J. M., R. Fus.
WADDILOVE, Pte. N., West Yorks.
WATSON, Sec.-Lt. W. V. C., W.Y.

Honours

CLARKE, Capt. A. A., Leicester Regt., M.C.
LING. Lt. W. H. G., M.C., R.A F

SMITH, Lt. G. S., Cambs. Rgt., M.C.
STANSFIELD, Capt. E. D., West Yorks., M.C.

COLLEGE OF THE RESURRECTION

Members who Joined the Forces

BATE, Lt. H. R., 2/6 Manch. Regt. att. 9 Royal Sussex
BROWN, Rev. C. G., Chaplain to Forces
BROWN, Sec.-Lt. F. C.
CROSS, Lt. and Adjt. Rev. E., 17 West Yorks. Regt.
EELES, Sec.-Lt. W. G., Worcester Regt. att. Chinese Labour Corps
FREESTONE, Rev. W. H., Chaplain to Forces
GROSER, Rev. ST. J. B., Chaplain to Forces
HARDING, Sec.-Lt. R., 6 Queens (R.W. Surrey)
HUKE, Sec.-Lt. H., R.E.
MONTGOMERY, Lt. G. E., Dorset Regt.
PERRY, Rev. R., Church Army France
RICHARDS, Rev. C. T., Chaplain to Forces
SMITH, Capt. F. W., West Yorks. Regt., G.S.O.
SUTCH, Rev. R. H., Chaplain to Forces
THORNEWILL, Capt. A. S., 2 North Staffs. att. S. & T. Corps, I.A.
WORSLEY, Lt. W. E., 1/8 West Yorks.

The Fallen

BROWN, Sec.-Lt. F. C.
FREESTONE, Rev. W. H., C.F., C.R.
HARDING, Sec.-Lt. REGINALD
MONTGOMERY, Lt. G. E.

Honours

BATE, Lt. H. R., M.C.
GROSER, Rev. ST. J. B., M.C., mentioned in despatches
HARDING, Sec.-Lt. R., M.C and bar
SMITH, Capt. F. W., M.C.
WORSLEY, Lt. W. E., M.C.

FREESTONE, REV. WILLIAM HERBERT C.R.
Chaplain to the Forces
Killed in action at Salonika December 14th 1916
College of the Resurrection

MONTGOMERY, GEORGE EDWARD
Lieutenant 5th Dorsetshire Regiment
Killed in action at Gallipoli August 1915
College of the Resurrection R.F.C.

DARNALL

Members who Joined the Forces

Ashworth, E.
Baker, G.
Carter, I.
Carter, J. L., 12 Y. & L.
Copley, A.
Green, M., Gym. Staff, Nrth. Fus.
Hall, Lt. B., Y. & L.
Hargreaves, T., 7 K.O.Y.L.I.
Higgins, Lt. F. R., 11 R.I.R. and 1/4 Y. & L.
Johnson, F., H.H.A.
Knighton, J., 12 Y. & L.
Main, Cpl. A., Nrth. Fus.
Philbey, Sgt. G., 12 Y. & L.

Rastrick, A. G.
Reeman, L., City of London Fus.
Register, B. J., 12 Y. & L.
Scarborough, H., 12 Y. & L.
Shipley, A.
Shipley, P.
Walker, Sgt. N., R.A.M.C.
Walker, Wireman D., H M.S. "Superb"
Wilford, L.-Cpl. C., 12 Y. & L.
Willford, J., 12 Y. & L.
Wilman, S.
Wolfe, A. G., Warwickshire Regt.

The Fallen

Ashworth, E.
Baker, G.
Copley, A.
Johnson, F.
Knighton, J.
Philbey, G.

Rastrick, A. G.
Register, B.
Scarborough, H.
Wilford, C.
Willford, J.
Wolfe, A. G.

COPLEY, ERNEST
Private 10th West Yorkshire Regiment
Killed on the Somme July 1st 1916
Darnall R.F.C.

KNIGHTON, J.
Sergeant 12th York and Lancaster Regiment
Killed in action July 1st 1916
Darnall R.F.C.

PHILBEY, G.
Sergeant 12th York and Lancaster Regiment
Killed in action July 1st 1916
Darnall R.F.C

RASTRICK, A. G.
Royal Marines
Died from operation after demobilisation
Darnall R.F.C.

WILLFORD, C.
Private 12th York and Lancaster Regiment (City Battalion Sheffield)
Died of wounds received July 1st 1916
Darnall R.F.C.

DONCASTER

Members who Joined the Forces

ABBISS, Lt. REG., West Yorks.
ANDERSON, Capt. R., R.A.M.C.
BATTIE-WRIGHTSON, R. C., A.S.C.
BRADLEY, Cpl., 1/6 K.O.Y.L.I.
BUTTON, —.
CARR, —.
CLARKE, Cpl. J. S., West Yorks.
COCKEY, Capt. W. H., K.O Y.L.I.
COMRIE, Lt. J.
COOK, Cpl. P., 15 West Yorks.
CROSLAND, Pte. J.
CROSLAND, Pte. W. G., M.G.C.
GRAY, Lt. D.
GRAYBOURN, —., Yorks. Drgns.
HARRISON, Sgt. E. A., K.R.R.
HEMINGWAY, Lt J., 1 Seaforth H.
HERD, Pte. B., R.E.
HETT, Lt.
HIRST, Sgt.
HOWSON, Sgt. F.
HOYLE, Capt. C. F., Notts. Yeo.
KEMP, Lt.
KIRKBY, Capt. F. O., R.F.A.
KNIGHT, —.
LLOYD-EVANS, R.S.M. J, A.S.C.
MACKAY, Surgeon Major P. B., Yorkshire Dragoons
MACOUN, S.M. J., R.E.
MACKAY, Capt. D. S., Indian Cav.
MANDERS, Capt. P. G.
McQUIRE, Lt. B., Irish Brigade
NETTLETON, W., Highland Regt.
OGLEY, Sgt., 6 K.O.Y.L.I.
PICKERING, Capt. B. H., K.O.Y.L.I.
PLUMMER, Lt., Manchester Regt.
REES, Acting Chaplain General Rev. GOWER
RICHARDSON, Capt.
ROBERTS, Lt. A. H.
ROBERTS, Lt. G. H., 2/4 K.O.Y.L.I.
ROBINSON, Pte. J., A.S.C.
RUSSELL, Lt
SEED, Lt. A. M.
SHARP, Major
SHARP, Lt. S. O., 12 Y. & L.
SIMONS, Capt. E., Camb. Unit
SMITH, Cpl. H. J., 4 Gordon H.
STEVENSON, Lt. R. L., R.A.F.
STEVENSON, Major D. F., R.A.F.
SUMMERS, Q.M. J., R.A.F.
TATHAM, Capt. B. M., 5 K.O.Y.L.I.
TUCKER, Capt. ALF, 5 K.O.Y.L.I.
WAITE, Sgt.
WALKER, Lt. A. T., 8 Rifle Brgd.
WALKER, Capt. J. W., 5 K.O.Y.L.I.
WHITEHEAD, —.
WILKINSON, Q.M. S. A., A.S.C.
WILLS, Capt. A. N., 5 K.O.Y.L.I.

The Fallen

ABBISS, Lt. REG.
BRADLEY, Cpl.
COMRIE, Lt. J.
COOK, Cpl. P.
GRAY, Lt. D.
HEMINGWAY, Lt. J.
HOWSON, Sgt. F.
McQUIRE, Lt. B.
OGLEY, Sgt.
ROBERTS, Lt. G. H.
RUSSELL, Lt.
SHARP, Lt. S. O.
TUCKER, Capt. A.
WALKER, Lt. A. T.
WALKER, Capt. J. W.
WHITEHEAD, —.
WILLS, Capt. A. N.

Honours

HERD, Pte. B., D.C.M.
HOWSON, Sgt. F., M.M.
HOYLE, Capt. C. F., M.C.
REES, Acting Chaplain General Rev. GOWER, M.C.
RICHARDSON, Capt., M.C., French decoration
ROBERTS, Lt. A. H., M.C., mentioned in despatches
SEED, Lt. A. M., M.C.
SHARP, Major, M.C. and Italian decoration, ment. in despatches
SIMONS, Capt. E., M.C. and bar, mentioned in despatches
STEVENSON, Major D. F., R.A.F., D.S.O.,M.C, ment. in despatches
STEVENSON, Lt. R. L., Croix de Guerre, mentioned in despatches

ABBISS, R. D.
2nd Lieutenant 2nd King's Own Yorkshire Light Infantry
Died of wounds December 2nd 1917
Doncaster R.F.C.

BRADLEY, W.
Corporal 1/6th King's Own Yorkshire Light Infantry
Killed on the Somme on or about September 1st 1918
Doncaster R.F.C.

COOK, PERCY
Lance-Corporal 15th West Yorkshire Regiment (Leeds Pals)
Killed Battle of the Somme July 1st 1917
Doncaster R.F.C.

HEMINGWAY, JAMES
2nd Lieutenant 1st Seaforth Highlanders
Killed in action May 9th 1915
Doncaster R.F.C.

OGLEY, —.
Sergeant 6th King's Own Yorkshire Light Infantry
Killed at Ypres September 7th 1915
Doncaster R.F.C.

ROBERTS, G. H.
Captain 2/4th King's Own Yorkshire Light Infantry (T.F.)
Died from wounds November 22nd 1917
Doncaster R.F.C.

SHARP, STEVE OSWALD
2nd Lieutenant 12th York and Lancaster Regiment
Killed in action near Serre July 1st 1916
Doncaster R.F.C.

TUCKER, ALF.
Captain 5th King's Own Yorkshire Light Infantry
Killed in action 1915
Doncaster R.F.C.

WALKER, ANTHONY T.
Lieutenant 8th Battalion Rifle Brigade
Killed in action at Hooge, Flanders, July 30th 1915
Doncaster R.F.C.

WALKER, JOHN WICKHAM
Captain 5th King's Own Yorkshire Light Infantry (T.F.)
Killed in action near Thiepval, France, July 5th 1916
Doncaster R.F.C.

WILLS, A. N.
Captain 5th King's Own Yorkshire Light Infantry
Died of wounds received at Ypres March 7th 1918
Doncaster R.F.C.

GIGGLESWICK SCHOOL

Members who Joined the Forces

AINLEY, Lt. F. C., Yorks. Regt.
ALLAWAY, Pte. W.
BARBER, Sec.-Lt. H. D., R.F.A.
BROOK, Capt. G., West Yorks. Rgt.
BROWN, G. K., West Yorks.
BROWNE, Lt. J. S., M.G.C.
CLUBB, J., R.A.F.
DOWNING, W., O.C.B. (Ind. Army)
FLEMING, Lt. W. R., R.S.F.
FOSTER, Lt. H., R.A.F.
FRANKLAND, V.
GIBSON, Lt. T. H., R.S.F.
GLAISTER, Pte. S., R.F.
HAGGAS, Sec.-Lt. J., R.F.A.
HALL, Sec.-Lt. M. T. R., R.F.A.
HAMILTON, Lt. A. S. L., R.F.A.
HANCOCK, Sub-Lt. J., R.N.A.S.
HEYS, Lt. J. H., East Lancs. Rgt.
HICKSON, Capt. S. H. V., West Yk.
HIGHAM, Sec.-Lt. F. S., R.F.A.
HORROCKS, Sec.-Lt. W. D. A., N.F.
HUNTER, Sec.-Lt. G. T. F., R.A.F.
JEPSON, Midshipman C. D., R.N.
KEMMIS-BETTY, Lt. W. M., R.G.A.
KENYON, Sec.-Lt. J. DE W.

KENYON, Lt. E. C., Cheshire Regt.
KING, Lt. A., West Riding Regt.
KINGSTON, S. T., O.C.B.
MAKINSON, Pte. G. R., Artists Rfls.
MURGATROYD, Lt. N. A., R.F.A.
NELSON, Lt. F. E., M.G.C.
PILLEY, Cadet H. C., R.E.
RAYNES, Capt. L., D.L.I.
ROBINSON, Cpl. C. E. M., D.L.I.
ROBINSON, Sec.-Lt. R. B., London Regt.
SAMES, Cadet A. R., O.C.B.
SHARP, Capt. D. G., West Yorks.
SLATER, Sec.-Lt. H., R.E.
SLATER, Pte. R., R.A.S.C.
SMITH, Cadet T. R. S., R.M.C.
TATTERSALL, Lt. F. G., Manch. R.
TAYLOR, Sec.-Lt. C. E., K.O.Y.L.I.
THOMAS, Sec.-Lt. J. L., R.F.A.
WHALEY, Lt. G. R., Tank Corps
WHARTON, Sec.-Lt. J. H., West Yk.
WILSON, Sec.-Lt. C., Gordon H.
WILSON, Sec.-Lt. K., R.E.
WORSWICK, Lt. R., R.F.A.

The Fallen

BROWN, Sec.-Lt. G. K., West Yks.
GLAISTER, Pte. S., R.F.

KENYON, Sec.-Lt. J. DE W.

Honours

BARBER, H. D., M.C.
FLEMING, W. R., M.C. and bar
HAMILTON, A. S. L., M.C.
HICKSON, S. H. V., mentioned in despatches

KEMMIS-BETTY, W. M., M.C.
KENYON, E. C., mentioned in despatches
SHARP, D. G., M.C.

GLAISTER, S.
Private Royal Fusiliers
Giggleswick School

HARROGATE OLD BOYS

Members who Joined the Forces

Appleby, Lt. N., Canadian Inf.
Appleyard, Capt. E. E., Yorks. R.
Appleyard, Lt. H. E., West Yks.
Ashby, Lt. A., Northants Yeo.
Atkinson, Capt. L. E., West Yks.
Atkinson, Capt. N. E., West Yks.
Atkinson, T., A.P.C.
Barret, Tpr. E., E. African M.R.
Barret, Capt. J. D., West Yorks.
Barrett, Sec.-Lt. N. K., West Yk.
Bastable, Capt. O., R.A.M.C.
Bergh, Major V. E. D., R.A.M.C.
Bland, Capt. H. S., West Yorks.
Bottomley, Lt. G. D. G., R.W.Sur.
Braithwaite, Major A. N., W.Y.
Chippindale, Sec.-Lt. C., R.F.A.
Claney, Lt. S. M., West Yorks.
Clubb, Lt. A. D., West Yorks.
Clubb, Capt. P., West Yorks.
Clubb, Lt. D. B., R.G.A.
Coggill, Cpl. H., West Yorks.
Collett, Gnr. F. W., R.F.A.
Crust, Cpl. W., West Yorks.
Davey, Lt. N., East Yorks.
Davey, Surg. Sub-Lt., J. M., R.N.V.R.
Dearden, Pte. R. S., Scot. Rifles
Dent, Sec.-Lt. G. R., R.F.A.
Drake, Lt. D., Indian Army
Duncan, Sec.-Lt. C. E., R.B.
Gibson, Ft.-Lt. W. F. G., R.A.F.
Gibson, Sec.-Lt. A. L., West Rdg.
Graves, Mechanic J. R., R.N.
Greathead, F.
Greenwood, Capt. J. J. G., W.Y.
Gregg, Staff-Sgt. G. H., R.A.S.C. (M.T.)
Harris, Capt. E.
Houston, Lt. T.
Howarth, Lt. J., A.I.F.
Jefferson, Lt.-Cmdr., R.N.

Kelley, Cpl. F., West Yorks.
Lawton, A. E.
Lewis, Pte. B., Canadian Inf.
Mantle, Capt. C. A., A.S.C.
Marston, Lt. F., R.E.
Milton, Capt. A. V., R.A.F.
Moxon, Lt. T. C., R.F.A.
Mutrie, Gnr. J. A., R.G.A.
Newstead, Sgt.-Major K. L., W.Y.
Pearson, Capt. C. H. M.
Pledge, Capt. E. K. M. De, W.Y.
Poole, Lt. W. J. R. E., Y. & L.
Raworth, Capt. R. G., R.E.
Rennard, Cpl. A., Canadian Inf.
Renton, Lt. E. G., R.A.S.C.
Roberts, Capt. H., K.O.Y.L.I.
Roberts, Sgt. W., West Yorks.
Robinson, Lt. N., R.A.F.
Sheffield, Capt. T. T. J., Tanks
Sheffield, Capt. W. L., R.A.V.C.
Simpson, Lt. T. C.
Simpson, Lt. J. M., R.E.
Simpson, Lt. G. W., A.I.F.
Slade, Lt. F., R.G.A.
Slade, A.-M. L., R.A.F.
Smith, Lt. A. F. L., West Yorks.
Stobart, Capt. R. F.
Storey, Sgt. C. W., Yorks. Hussars
Storey, Capt. K., D.L.I.
Strother, Capt. T. L. W., Tanks
Strother, Lt. J. M., Y. & L.
Tucker, Pte. F., West Yorks.
Tucker, Capt. A., K.O.Y.L.I.
Verity, Lt. K., R.F.A.
Voakes, Tpr. W., Yorks. Hussars
Watson, D. J.
Watson, Surg. Sub-Lt. C. Riley, R.N.V.R.
Watson, Lt. L. Riley
Wilson, Lt., West Yorks.
Wilson, Lt. D. J., Yorks. Regt.

HARROGATE OLD BOYS—*continued*

THE FALLEN

APPLEBY, Lt. N.
APPLEYARD, Lt. H. E.
ATKINSON, Capt. L. E.
COGGILL, Cpl. H.
CRUST, Cpl. W.
DEARDEN, Pte. R. S.
DUNCAN, Sec.-Lt. C. E.
GIBSON, Sec.-Lt. A. L.
HARRIS, Capt. E.
KELLEY, Cpl. F.
LAWTON, A. E.

MOXON, Lt. T. C.
PLEDGE, Capt. E. K. M. DE
POOLE, Lt. W. J. R. E.
RENTON, Lt. E. G.
SIMPSON, Lt. J. M.
SIMPSON, Lt. G. W.
STROTHER, Lt. J. M.
TUCKER, Pte. F.
TUCKER, Capt. A.
WATSON, Lt. L. RILEY
WATSON, D. J.

HONOURS

APPLEBY, Lt. W., M.M. and bar
APPLEYARD, Capt. E. E., M.C.
ATKINSON, Capt. N. E., mentioned in despatches
BRAITHWAITE, Major A. N., D.S.O. M.C.
CLUBB, Lt. D. B., Croix de Guerre
GREENWOOD, Capt. J. J. G., mentioned in despatches

HOUSTON, Lt. T., M.C.
RENNARD, Cpl. A., M.M.
ROBERTS, Capt. H., Croix de Guerre
SIMPSON, Lt. T. C., M.C.
SIMPSON, Lt. J. M., mentioned in despatches
STOREY, Capt. K., M.C.
STROTHER Lt. J. M., M.C.

APPLEBY, NORMAN, M.M. and Bar
Lieutenant 31st Canadian Infantry
Killed near Neuville St. Vaast on March 29th 1917
Harrogate Old Boys

APPLEYARD, HARRY ELSTON
2nd Lieutenant 12th West Yorkshire Regiment
Killed in action at Bazentin-le-Grand, France, July 16th 1916
Sedbergh School and Harrogate Old Boys

ATKINSON, LAURIE EVANS
Captain 3rd West Yorkshire Regiment
Killed in action April 20th 1916
Harrogate Old Boys and Sedbergh

COGGILL, HAROLD
Corporal 15th West Yorkshire Regiment
Killed 1st July 1916
Harrogate Old Boys

DEARDON, REGINALD S.
Private Cameronians (1st Scottish Rifles)
Killed in action on the Somme at High Wood July 16th 1916
Harrogate Old Boys

DUNCAN, C. ERIC
2nd Lieutenant 3rd Battalion Rifle Brigade
Killed in action at Loos November 24th 1917
Harrogate Old Boys

GIBSON, ARTHUR LIONEL
2nd Lieutenant 1/7th Duke of Wellington's West Riding Regiment
Killed at Pilkem, Belgium, August 8th 1915
Harrogate Old Boys

KELLEY, FRED
Corporal 1/5th West Yorkshire Regiment
Died of wounds July 15th 1915
Harrogate Old Boys

MOXON, TOM CYRIL
Lieutenant 311th Brigade Royal Field Artillery
Died November 19th 1918
Harrogate Old Boys

POOLE, WILLIAM JOHN ROWLAND ERNEST
Lieutenant 3/4th York and Lancaster Regiment
Fell in action October 9th 1917
Harrogate Old Boys

PLEDGE, E. K. M. DE
Captain 15th West Yorkshire Regiment
Killed in action
Harrogate Old Boys

RENTON, E. G.
Lieutenant Royal Army Service Corps
Died at Lahore, India, May 29th 1918 while on active service
Harrogate Old Boys

SIMPSON, JAMES M.
2nd Lieutenant
Killed in action May 9th 1916
Harrogate Old Boys

SIMPSON, GEORGE
Lieutenant Australian Imperial Force
Killed in France August 23rd 1918
Harrogate Old Boys

STROTHER, J. M., M.C.
2nd Lieutenant York and Lancaster Regiment
Killed in action April 28th 1917
Harrogate Old Boys

TUCKER, FRED E.
Private 15th West Yorkshire Regiment (Leeds Pals)
Killed July 1st 1916 at the Battle of the Somme
Harrogate Old Boys

WATSON, LESLIE RILEY
2nd Lieutenant West Riding Brigade Royal Field Artillery
Killed at Thiepval July 4th 1916
Harrogate Old Boys

HEADINGLEY

Members who Joined the Forces

AHEARN, Capt., R.A.M.C.
ALLISON, Lt. G. F., West Riding
AMPT, W.
AMPT, Lt. N. C., 1 Border Regt.
ANDERSON, Sec.-Lt. A. E., D.L.I.
ARMITAGE, Major J. A. R., 15 W.Y.
ARMITAGE, Capt. A. W., 8 K.O.Y.L.I.
AUTY, Lt. J. S., 16 West Yorks.
BARBER, Lt. S., R.F.A.
BATTLE, Capt. A. E., 7 West Yks.
BATTLE, Lt. C. H., A.S.C.
BEALE, Capt. and Adj. C. V., 1/7 West Yorks.
BEASLEY, Lt. R. N., Manch. Regt.
BELK, C. G.
BELL, J. G.
BENNETT, Lt. W. D., R.G.A.
BLENCOWE, Lt. L. C., Liverpool Sc.
BLENCOWE, Lt. O. C., Royal Fus.
BOTTOMLEY, Sec.-Lt. W. E., 3/1 Lowland Division
BOTTOMLEY, Lt. A. E., Black Wch.
BOYLE, Lt. P., Labour Corps
BOYLE, Lt. JAMES, R.E.
BOYLE, Capt. A., R.A.M.C.
BRADLEY, Bd. W. P., R.F.A.
BRINDLEY, Gnr. R., R.F.A.
BROWN, Sec.-Lt. H. R., W.R. How.
BROWN, Sec.-Lt. W. R., 8 West Yk.
BROWN, Lt. N. B. R., Ass. Billeting Officer, B.R.G.
BROWN, H. C., A.S.C.
BROWN, EVANS
BUCHANAN, Cpl. D., R.A.M.C.
CALVERT, Capt. R. C., 7 West Yks.
CALVERT, Lt. G. C., K.O.Y.L.I.
CALVERT, Pte. J. C., 5 Can. R.H.
CALVERT, Capt. E. E., 7 East Yks.
CAMPBELL, Lt. W. A., R.A.F.
CARLYLE, Lt. ROBT., 1/5 K.O.S.B.
CAUTHERLEY, Lt. G. H., A.S.C.
COGHLAN, Lt. W. H., R.F.A.
COOPER, Lt. F. T., 12 Y. & L.
CORK, Sec.-Lt. S., Yorks. Regt.
DAWSON, Lt. G. H. W., 15 West Y.
DAWSON, Lt. H., R.F.A.
DAWSON, Sec.-Lt. W. F., 16 W.Y.
DEAKIN, Lt. J. P., 3/2 Mon. Regt.
DENTON, Capt. F., R.E.
DIXON, Major S. C., R.F.A.

DOBSON, Lt.-Col. J. F., R.A.M.C. 2 Northern General
DOBSON, Lt. R. C., R.G.A.
DOWNES, Cpl. H. F., Yorks. Huss.
EASTWOOD, Sec.-Lt. H., 31 Trench Mortars
EDDISON, Capt. J. H., R.F.A.
EDWARDS, Bd. N. S., R.G.A.
EVANS, W. D. L.
EWBANK, Rev. H., Chaplain
FECHT, L. B.
FLESHER, Lt. H., R.E.
FLESHER, Sec.-Lt. F. A., 2/6 Wark.
FLETCHER, Sec.-Lt. E. S., 2/6 W.Y.
FLETCHER, A. E.
FOIZEY, Lt. H. E., 16 West Yorks.
FOORD, Lt. GEO., D Btty., R.H.A.
FORBES, Capt. E., R.A.M.C.
FOXTON, Lt. H., 2 W.R. Fld. Amb.
FIRTH, Cpl. D. A., West Yorks.
FRANK, Capt. R., R.G.A.
FRANK, Lt. R. V., A.S.C.
FRANK, —.
FRANKLYN, Capt. H. C., 2 Yorks.
GAILLE, Sgt. E., Australian Forces
GELDER, Pte. F., York & Lancs.
GELDER, Lt. G. R., Welsh Regt.
GREATHEAD, Lt. A. M., S.A. Eng.
GREATHEAD, Lt. J. M., S.A. Eng.
HAMILTON, Lt. A. S., 15 West Yks.
HAMILTON, Capt. J. S., 2/7 W.Y.
HAMILTON, Lt. T., 2/7 West Yorks.
HAMILTON, Lt. D., 11 West Yorks.
HAMMOND, Capt. G. H., 8 West Y.
HAMMOND, Lt. A. J., Australian F.
HEPWORTH, Lt. C., R.F.C.
HEPWORTH, Lt. J., M.T.A.C.
HICKSON, Lt. J. L., 19 D.L.I.
HILTON, Gnr. J., R.F.A.
HINDLE, Sec.-Lt. E. V., K.O.Y.L.1.
HININGS, Capt. F. W., 3 East Yks.
HODGSON, Lt. J. H. C., 3/8 W.Y.
HOFFMANN, Lt. S. L. F., 16 W.Y.
HOLMES, Capt. J. M., R.F.A.
HOYLE, Capt. C. F., R.F.C.
HUDSON, Major W., R.E
HUNTER, Capt. S. A., 3/4 West Yk.
HUTCHINSON, Sgt.-Major H., 2 Lancaster Hussars
HUTCHINSON, Lt. F., R.G.A.
IBBITSON, Sgt.-Farr. E. D., H.A.C.

HEADINGLEY—continued

MEMBERS WHO JOINED THE FORCES—continued

IBBITSON, Lt. T. C., R.F.A.
INGHAM, Major H., 1 West Yorks.
JACKSON, Lt. S. F., 7 West Yorks.
JACKSON, Sec.-Lt. C., R.G.A.
JAMESON, Lt. H., 2/1 Yorks. Drgs.
JAMESON, Lt. J. L., 1/5 West Yks.
JAMESON, Lt. C. N., 3/4 Lincoln R.
JAMESON, Major H. A., R.F.A.
JEFFERSON, Lt. I. S., R.N.
JOHNSON, Lt. W., 4 Royal Fus.
JOHNSON, Lt. S., 2/7 West Yorks.
KENDALL, Major J. F., R.E.
KENNINGTON, Lt. F. R., 19 W.Y.
KIDD, Major N. V., West Riding
KILPATRICK, Lt. & Adj. G.H., R.F.A.
KING, L.-Cpl. J. A., Liverpool Scot.
KING, Bd. A., 4 W.R. R.F.A.
KING, Lt. P. J., R.F.A.
KING, Pte. B., West Yorks.
KNOWLES, Lt. C., R.N.A.S.
KNOWLES, Lt. J., 11 Y. & L.
KNOWLES, Sec.-Lt. F. E., 11 Y. & L.
LEE, H., South African Forces
LEE, Sgt. E., 1 Auck., N.Z. Forces
LIDDELL, Adj. G. C., Q.M.G. Headquarters Staff, 1 Army Corps
LILLEY, Capt. H. H., 2 Yorks. Rgt.
LITTLE, Lt. H. E., 3/1 Sherwood R.
LONGBOTTOM, Major T., 3/8 W.Y.
LUMB, Cpl. T. D., Yorks. Hussars
LUPTON, Capt. L. M., 8 West Yks.
MACLAREN, W., Canadian R.F.A.
MACPHERSON, Lt. A. S., R.A.M.C.
MAGEE, Capt. D. H., 2 Yorks. Rgt.
MARSHALL, Capt. D. V., R.A.F.
MIDGLEY, Sec.-Lt. E. R., 1/5 K.O.Y.L.I.
MILLS, Pte. J. W., 18 West Yorks.
MOIR, Lt. L. R., D Cornwall's L.I.
MOTLEY, Lt. A. H. L., East Yorks.
MYERS, Capt. E., 3/6 West Yorks.
NICHOLSON, Sq.-Cm. W. E., R.A.F.
NICHOLSON, Sec.-Lt. R. M., R.F.A.
NUTT, Lt. D. L., R.A.F.
OAKES, Lt. W. L., 13 D.L.I.
OLDHAM, Capt. H., 15 West Yorks.
PARKES, Sec.-Lt. H., R.E.
PEACOCK, Lt. H. P., A.S.C.
PICKLES, Sgt. H. D., 15 West Yks.
PLATTS, Lt. J. E. A., R.F.A.
POTTS, Sig. C., R.G.A.
RAMSDEN, Lt. E., 3 West Yorks.
REDMAN, Lt. W., 15 West Yorks.
REDMAYNE, Major J. B., West Yks.
REID, Sec.-Lt. A., 1/22 London Rg. (The Queen's)
RHODES, Lt. J. R., R.F.A.
RHODES, Lt. J., 6 West Yorks.
RIDDETT, Capt. S. A., R.A.M.C.
RIGBY, Lt. L. W., 7 West Yorks.
RIMMER, S.S.M. R., A.S.C.
ROBINSON, Major H., A.S.C. (M.T.)
ROBINSON, Capt. H. I., R.W. Kent
ROBINSON, Lt. M., M.G.C.
ROBINSON, Pte. J., W.R. Fld. Amb.
ROBISON, Sgt. W. A., R.F.A.
SHARP, Pte. F. R., 15 West Yorks.
SHAW, Lt. F. M., R.F.A.
SHAW, Lt. C. P., 1 Sherwood Rang.
SMEETH, Lt. W. S., R.A.F.
STOCKDALE, Lt. C. A., R.F.A.
STOCKWELL, Major Dr. E. J. ST. CLAIRE, R.A.M.C.
SWAINE, Bd. A. B., R.G.A.
TANSLEY, V.
TARR, Capt. and Adj. F. N. Leicester Regt.
TETLOW, Sec.-Lt. A. L., R.F.A.
THOMAS, Lt. A. H., R.A.S.C.
THOMPSON, Capt. J. T. L.
TOWNSLEY, Lt. H. A., R.A.F.
TUCKETT, H. E.
TWENTYMAN, Capt. D. C. T., Y. & L.
VAUSE, Lt. J. G., 15 West Yorks.
WALKER, H. M. B.
WALKER, Lt. H. G., 3 K.O.Y.L.I.
WATERHOUSE, Sec.-Lt. R. B. M. 5 Reserve West Yorks.
WATSON, Ft.-Lt. K. F., R.N.A.S.
WELLS, Lt. D. S., 15 West Yorks.
WHITAKER, Lt. C. F., 1 W. Riding
WHITAKER, Capt. CLIFFORD, 15 West Yorks.
WHITAKER, Sgt. HARPER, Nigerian Regt., East African Exped. Fce.
WHITAKER, H. B.
WHITE, Lt. H. J., 1/10 Liverpool Scottish
WHITE, Major F. W., R.F.A.
WILSON, J., 5 Canadian Royal H.
WOLSTENHOLME, Cpl. F., 15 W.Y.
WOLSTENHOLME, Cpl. J., R.E. (Sig. Section)
WOOD, Lt. A. N. G., 21 West Yks.

HEADINGLEY—continued

The Fallen

Ampt, N. C.
Armitage, A. W.
Blencowe, L. C.
Blencowe, O. C.
Brindley, R.
Brown, W. R.
Calvert, R. C.
Calvert, J. C.
Calvert, G. C.
Campbell, W. A.
Carlyle, R.
Coghlan, W. H.
Dawson, H. H. M.
Flesher, F. A.
Fletcher, E. S.
Frank, —.
Gaille, E.
Hamilton, T.
Hinings, F. W.
Ingham, H.
Jackson, S. F.
Jameson, J. L.
Jameson, H. A.
Jefferson, I. S.

Kidd, N. V.
King, P. J.
King, J. A.
Lumb, T. D.
Lupton, L. M.
Midgley, E. R.
Mills, J. W.
Pickles, H. D.
Reid, A.
Robison, W. A.
Sharp, F. R.
Smeeth, W. S.
Tarr, F. N.
Thompson, J. T. L.
Townsley, H. A.
Twentyman, D. C. T.
Vause, J. G.
Walker, H. G.
Waterhouse, R. B. M.
Watson, K.
Whitaker, G. C.
Whitaker, H.
Whitaker, C. F.

Honours

Bottomley, A. E., D.C.M.
Brown, W. R., M.C.
Dobson, R. C., M.C.
Eddison, J. H., M.C.
Edwards, N., M.M.
Forbes, E., M.C.
Frank, R., Croix de Guerre, Croix de Chevalier de la Couronne
Franklyn, Capt. (Brevet Major), D.S.O., M.C.
Hamilton, J. S., D.S.O.
Hamilton, T., M.B.E.

Hudson, W., O.B.E.
Ingham, H., M.C.
Jameson, J. L., M.C.
Jameson, H. A., M.C. and bar
Jefferson, J. S., Humane Soc. M.
Kidd, N. V., M.C.
King, P. T., M.M.
Liddell, G. C., D.S.O.
Lilley, Capt. H. H. (Tempy. Lt.-Col.), D.S.O.
Myers, E., M.C.
Rhodes, J. Reg., D.C.M.

AMPT, NORMAN CROSLAND
2nd Lieutenant Border Regiment
Killed at Suvla Bay August 21st 1915
Headingley R.F.C.

BLENCOWE, L. C.
Lieutenant 1/10th Liverpool Scottish
Killed in action at Bois Grenier June 1917
Headingley R.F.C.

BROWN, W. R., M.C.
Lieutenant 2/7th West Yorkshire Regiment
Killed at Grandcourt November 21st 1917
Headingley R.F.C.

BRINDLEY, R.
Gunner Royal Field Artillery
Killed near Ypres June 3rd 1917
Headingley R.F.C.

CALVERT, J. C.
Private 5th Canadian Royal Highlanders
Missing first gas attack Battle of Ypres April 22nd 1915
Headingley R.F.C.

CALVERT, R. C.
Captain 7th West Yorkshire Regiment
Died of wounds near Poperinghe July 15th 1916
Headingley R.F.C.

CALVERT, G. C.
Lieutenant King's Own Yorkshire Light Infantry
Died at Mauberge January 15th 1919
Headingley R.F.C.

CAMPBELL, W. A.
Lieutenant 1/7th West Yorkshire Regiment attached to Royal Flying Corps
Died of wounds in France September 22nd 1917
Leeds Grammar School and Headingley R.F.C.

CARLYLE, R.
Lieutenant 5th King's Own Scottish Borderers
Killed at Gallipoli July 12th 1915
Headingley R.F C.

DAWSON, HERBERT HENRY MAWSON
2nd Lieutenant Royal Field Artillery
Killed July 19th 1916
Headingley R.F.C.

FLETCHER, E. STEWART
2nd Lieutenant 2/6th West Yorkshire Regiment
Missing and presumed killed at Bullecourt May 3rd 1917
Headingley R.F.C.

GAILLE, E.
Sergeant Australian Contingent
Killed at the Dardenelles August 7th 1915
Headingley R.F.C.

HAMILTON, TOM
2nd Lieutenant 2/7th West Yorkshire Regiment
Wounded and missing May 14th 1917
Headingley R.F.C.

HININGS, F. W.
Captain 3rd East Yorkshire Regiment
Killed near Gendecourt, in the Somme Battle, September 25th 1916
Headingley R.F.C.

INGHAM, HORACE, M.C.
Major 1st West Yorkshire Regiment
Killed April 1918
Headingley R.F.C.

JACKSON, S. F.
Lieutenant 1/7th West Yorkshire Regiment
Killed November 17th 1917
Headingley R.F.C.

JAMESON, H. A., M.C. and Bar
Major Royal Field Artillery
March 24th 1918, Misery-sur-Somme
Headingley R.F.C.

JAMESON, J. L., M.C.
Lieutenant 1/5th West Yorkshire Regiment
Killed at Thiepval Ridge July 2nd 1916
Headingley R.F.C.

JEFFERSON, INGLEBY STUART
Lieutenant Royal Navy
Killed in action when in command of H.M. Submarine C34 in the
North Sea July 21st 1917
United Services and Headingley R.F.C.

KING, J. A.
Lance-Corporal Liverpool Scottish
Missing August 9th 1916
Headingley R.F.C.

KING, P. J.
2nd Lieutenant Royal Field Artillery
Killed at Ypres salient October 24th 1917
Headingley R.F.C.

LUMB, T. D.
Corporal Yorkshire Hussars
Killed at Ypres May 25th 1915
Headingley R.F.C.

MIDGLEY, E. REGINALD
2nd Lieutenant 1/5th King's Own Yorkshire Light Infantry
Killed in action near Ypres November 16th 1915
Headingley R.F.C.

MILLS, J. W.
Private 18th West Yorkshire Regiment
Killed on the Somme July 1st 1916
Headingley R.F.C.

PICKLES, HERBERT GLADSTONE
Sergeant 15th West Yorkshire Regiment
Presumed killed in action May 3rd 1917
Headingley R.F.C.

REID, A.
2nd Lieutenant 1/22nd London Regiment (The Queen's)
Killed in action at Hill 60, near Ypres, February 15th 1917
Headingley R.F.C.

SHARP, F. R.
Private 15th West Yorkshire Regiment
Killed July 1st 1916
Headingley R.F.C.

SMEETH, W. S.
Lieutenant Royal Irish Rifles afterwards transferred to Royal Flying Corps
Killed July 17th 1917
Headingley R.F.C.   Fettes-Loretto Old Boys, also member of Bradford Cricket Club and played for the Yorkshire County 2nd XI.

TARR, F. N.
Lieutenant 4th Leicestershire Regiment
Headingley R.F.C.

TOWNSLEY, H. ALAN
2nd Lieutenant Royal Air Force
Killed at Courtreau on October 14th 1918
Headingley R.F.C.

TWENTYMAN, DENZIL CLIVE TATE
Captain York and Lancaster Regiment
Killed in the battle of the Somme July 1st 1916
Headingley R.F.C.

VAUSE, JOHN GILBERT
Lieutenant (acting Captain) 15th West Yorkshire Regiment
Killed in action at the battle of the Somme July 1st 1916
Headingley R.F.C.

WALKER, H. GERALD
2nd Lieutenant King's Own Yorkshire Light Infantry
Killed at Theipval July 1st 1916
Headingley R.F.C.

WATERHOUSE, ROBERT BENTLEY-MASKILL
2nd Lieutenant 5th Reserve West Yorkshire Regiment
Died in hospital March 26th 1919, result of injuries received in train smash at Cambrai on October 13th 1918
Headingley R.F.C.

WATSON, KENNETH FALSHAW
Flight-Lieutenant Royal Naval Air Service
Missing August 3rd 1915
Headingley R.F.C.

WHITAKER, CLIFFORD
Captain 15th West Yorkshire Regiment
Killed July 1st 1916
Headingley R.F.C.

WHITAKER, C. F.
Lieutenant West Riding Regiment
Killed at Hill 60, Belgium, May 6th 1915
Headingley R.F.C.

WHITAKER, T. H.
Sergeant Nigerian Regiment (East African Expeditionary Force)
Died of enteric fever in German East Africa January 9th 1918
Headingley R.F.C.

HUDDERSFIELD OLD BOYS

Members who Joined the Forces

AINLEY, Lt. W. H. S., 8 West Rdg.
ASHWORTH, Major W.
BEADON, Capt. B. S., 7 Welsh Fus.
BECKWITH, Lt. J., 7 West Riding
BLACKBURN, Lt. J., R.F.A.
BLETCHER, Capt. T., 10 Manch. Regt.
BRADLEY, Sgt. H., R.A.M.C.
CLIFFORD, Capt. G., 7 West Riding
CLIFFORD, Gnr. F. H., R.F.A.
CUTHBERT, Lt. M., R.N.R.
DAVIES, Lt.
FIELDHOUSE, Sgt. H., M.G.C.
FIELDHOUSE, Petty-Off. E., R.N.D.
FLAXINGTON, Lt.
HADDON, Lt. R., 4 West Riding
HARGREAVES, Capt. I., 7 West Rdg.
HARTLEY, Lt. J. A., 4 West Riding
HIRST, Sgt. E. P. K.
INGHAM, Capt. H., 5 West Riding
IRONS, Lt. E. A., R.G.A.
KERSHAW, Pte. C., Coldstream Gd.
LINDLEY, Sgt. S., 5 West Riding
MELLOR, Pte. A., R.F.A.
MORRELL, Sgt. H., R.A.M.C.
NETHERWOOD, Capt. H. S., 7 West Riding Regt.
OWEN, Lt. R., 2 West Riding
PEARSON, Cpl. J., R.G.A.
PRYNN, Lt., 10 West Riding
REA, Sgt. W., Welsh Borderers
RAMSDEN, Capt. J. W., 7 West R.
RILEY, Lt. T., 4 West Riding
RIPPON, Lt. N., 5 West Riding
SCHOFIELD, Lt. W., R.N.
SCOTT, Lt. W. A., R.G.A.
STANSFIELD, Lt.
SYKES, Petty-Off. H., R.N.
TAYLOR, Capt. N., R.F.A.
THORNTON, Lt. F., 7 East Yorks.
WARD, Lt. J. S., A.O.C.
WILDBLOOD, Lt. W., A.S.C.
WOODHEAD, Lt. H. M., 9 West Rdg.
WOOLVEN, Capt. S., 7 West Riding

The Fallen

BEADON, Capt. B. S.
HARTLEY, Lt. J. A.
OWEN, Lt. R. H.
REA, Sgt. W.
RILEY, Lt. T.
RIPPON, Lt. N.
THORNTON, Lt. F.
WILDBLOOD, Lt. W.

Honours

ASHWORTH, Major W., M.C.
BLETCHER, Capt. T., M.C.
NETHERWOOD, Capt. H. S., M.C.
TAYLOR, Capt. N., M.C.

BEADON, BASIL HERBERT E.
Captain and Adjutant 7th Royal Welsh Fusiliers
Killed in action at Suvla Bay August 10th 1915
Huddersfield Old Boys

HARTLEY, J. A.
2nd Lieutenant 4th Duke of Wellington's West Riding Regiment
Suffocated by gas on December 19th 1915
Huddersfield Old Boys

OWEN, ROWLAND HELY
Lieutenant 3rd Duke of Wellington's Regiment
Killed April 18th 1915
Huddersfield Old Boys

REA, W. J.
Sergeant 11th South Wales Borderers
Killed July 7th 1916
Huddersfield Old Boys

RILEY, J. TREVOR
Lieutenant 4th Duke of Wellington's West Riding Regiment
Killed September 3rd 1916
Huddersfield Old Boys

RIPPON, N. H.
2nd Lieutenant 5th Duke of Wellington's Regiment
Killed November 18th 1915
Huddersfield Old Boys

THORNTON, F.
2nd Lieutenant 7th East Yorkshire Regiment
Killed July 1st 1916
Huddersfield Old Boys

WILDBLOOD, W. A.
Lieutenant 195th Company Army Service Corps
Killed in Flanders June 16th 1917
Huddersfield Old Boys

HULL AND EAST RIDING

Members who Joined the Forces

ALLEN, Lt. T. G., East Yorks.
ATKINSON, Lt. D., East Yorks.
BRAITHWAITE, Dvr. G. W., M.T.
BURBIDGE, Lt. J. C., Rifle Brigade
CARGILL, Capt. A., R.F.A.
CARGILL, Capt. E., East Yorks.
CHALTON, Pte C. D., Field Ambce.
CLARKE, Lt. H. D., R.G.A.
DIBB, Capt. R. K., East Yorks.
FELLOWES, C.Q.M.S. A., R.G.A.
FISHER, Major J. L., Australian I.
FREEBOROUGH, Capt. M., Oxford Y.
GIBSON, Capt. B. K., East Yorks.
HALL, Lt. A. B., East Yorks.
HARTLEY, Lt. a/Major A. C., R.A.F.
HILLERNS, Capt. a/Major O. H. W. R.F.A.
HOLLIS, Lt. G. T., East Yorks.
HOPKINSON, Lt. H., R.E.
HUTCHINSON, Capt. F. H., 121 Labour Corps, Indian Army
HUTCHINSON, Capt. A. H., K.O.Y.L.I.
HUTCHINSON, Major W. H., R.F.A.
INGLEBY, Major C. J., East Yorks.
INGLEBY, Capt. N. W., East Yks.
JOHNSON, C. H.
KITCHING, Capt. a/Lt.-Col. J. E. R.E.
LACEY, Dvr. C. H., M.T.
LAMBERT, Capt. G., East Yorks.
LAMBERT, Lt. S. C., East Yorks.
LAVERACK, Capt. E., East Yorks.
MACILWAINE, Capt. a/Major A. H. R.H.A.
MACILWAINE, Capt. H. L., Midd. R.
MACILWAINE, Lt. G. W., 12 Lancers
MACILWAINE, Lt. a/Capt. A. A. M., 18 Hussars
MACKRILL, O. W., R.A.F.
MACNAMARA, Lt. H. C., R.F.A.
MAJOLIER, Lt. a/Capt., Yorks. R.
MUNGALL, Lt. R. H., Cavalry Res.
PEARCE, Lt.-Col. C., Yorks. Regt.
PIERSON, Lt. V. M., R.F.A.
QUIBELL, Major S. B., East Yorks.
REDFERN, Capt. J., East Yorks. and Staff
REDFERN, Capt. W., East Yorks.
RHODES, Pte. A., Canadian Artlly.
ROBINSON, Capt. a/Major T., R.F.A.
RUSSELL, F. A.
SEED, Capt. H. N., East Yorks.
SIMPSON, Lt. G. G., M.G.C.
STAINFORTH, Lt. G.
STOREY, Lt. W. R., R.G.A.
SYKES, Lt.Col. Sir MARK, Yorks. R.
THORP, Capt. N. A., K.O.S.B.
WADE, Major H. F., R.F.A.
WARD, Major G., R.F.A.
WATERHOUSE, Pte. A., London Rg.
WATERHOUSE, Cpl. K., M.T.
WATSON, Capt. G. H., R.A.M.C.
WATSON, Lt. A. E., M.G.C.
WATT, Lt. G., East Yorks.
WHITTICK, Bomb. T., R.F.A.
WILLIAMS, Lt. L. R., R.F.A.
WILSON, Lt.-Col. CLIVE, East Riding Yeomanry
WILSON, D.

HULL AND EAST RIDING—continued

THE FALLEN

ALLEN, Lt. T. G., East Yorks.
CHALTON, Pte. C. D., E. Lanc. F.A.
HALL, Lt. A. B., East Yorks.
HILLERNS, Capt. a/Major O. H. W., R.F.A.
HOPKINSON, Lt. H., R.E.
INGLEBY, Capt. N. W., East Yorks.
JOHNSON, C H.

MAJOLIER, Lt. a/Capt., Yorks. R.
QUIBELL, Major S. B., East Yorks.
REDFERN, Capt. W., East Yorks.
RHODES, Pte. A., Canadian Artlly.
STAINFORTH, Lt. G.
WATSON, Capt. G. H., R.A.M.C.
WILLIAMS, Lt. L. R., R.F.A.
WILSON, D.

HONOURS

ATKINSON, Major A. J., O.B.E.
HUTCHINSON, Major W. H. H., M.C.
INGLEBY, Major C. J., D.S.O.
LAMBERT, Capt. GUY, M.C.
MACILWAINE, Capt. a/Major A. H. D.S.O., M.C., Croix de Guerre
MACILWAINE, Lt. a/Capt. A. A. M. M.C.

PEARCE, Lt.-Col. CYRIL, O.B.E.
REDFERN, Capt. J., D.S.O.
ROBINSON, Capt. a/Major T., M.C.
SEED, Capt. H. N., M.C.
STOREY, Lt. W. R., M.B.E.
WILSON, Lt.-Col. CLIVE, D.S.O.

ALLEN, T. G.
Lieutenant East Yorkshire Regiment
Killed in action May 27th 1918
Hull and East Riding R.F.C.

CHALTON, G. D.
Private 3/1st East Lancashire Field Artillery
Captured March 21st 1918. Died at Aachen Hospital October 28th 1918.
Hull and East Riding R.F.C.

HALL, A. B.
Lieutenant 11th East Yorkshire Regiment
Killed in action May 3rd 1918
Hull and East Riding R.F.C.

HILLERNS, H. W. O.
Captain acting Major Royal Field Artillery
Killed in action
Hull and East Riding R.F.C.

HOPKINSON, H.
Lieutenant Royal Engineers
Killed in action
Hull and East Riding

INGLEBY, N. W.
Captain 4th East Yorkshire Regiment (T.F.)
Killed in action May 27th 1918
Hull and East Riding R.F.C.

MAJOLIER, E.
Lieutenant 5th Yorkshire Regiment
Died of pneumonia contracted on active service November 26th 1918
Hull and East Riding R.F.C.

QUIBELL, S. B.
Major East Yorkshire Regiment (T.F.)
Killed in action
Hull and East Riding R.F.C.

REDFERN, W.
Lieutenant (Acting Captain) 3rd East Yorkshire Regiment
Killed in action
Hull and East Riding R.F.C.

RHODES, A.
Private 29th (Vancouver Battalion) Canadians
Killed in action April 6th 1916
Hull and East Riding R.F.C.

STAINFORTH, G.
2nd Lieutenant 13th King's Liverpool Regiment
Killed in action July 14th 1916
Hull and East Riding R.F.C.

WATSON, G. H.
Captain Royal Army Medical Corps (T.F.)
3rd Northumbrian Field Ambulance
Died of wounds received in action September 18th 1916
Hull and East Riding R.F.C.

WILLIAMS, LEIGH ROSLIN
Lieutenant Royal Field Artillery (T.F.)
Killed in action May 27th 1918
Hull and East Riding R.F.C.

HYMERS COLLEGE

Members who Joined the Forces

Bilham, Capt. and Adj. D. G. R. 2 West Riding
Bilham, Lt. S. E. G., West Riding
Dick, Lt. A. K., R.A.S.C.
England, Lt. E. W., K.O.Y.L.I.
Forbes, Lt. J. S., R.G.A.
Forty, Sec.-Lt. F. J., R.A.F.
Green, Gnr. P. V., R.G.A.
Hagues, G., R.A.F.
Helmsing, Lt. E. F., East Yorks.
Hodgson, Prob. Surg. T. B., R.N.
Hollis, Lt. J. A., R.A.F.
Hollis, Sec.-Lt. H. R., East Yks.
Hutton, Pte. J. H., Northd. Fus.
Jarman, Ft.-Lt. R., R.A.F.
Jarman, Sec.-Lt. M., R.A.F.
Laverack, Capt. E., East Yorks.
Milner, E.
Peckett, Gnr. C., H.A.C.
Richardson, Lt. R. E., R.G.A.
Rishworth, K., R.A.F.
Simpson, Pte. H. G. S., 6 Midd. Rg.
Smith, H. A.
Stephenson, Sap. R., R.E.
Stewart, Sec.-Lt. G., West Riding
Walker, Pte. C. N., 21 K.R.R.
Watson, Lt. J. C., Middlesex Rgt.
Webb, C. A.
Weightman, Sec.-Lt. H., R.A.F.
Whittle, Sap. C. J., R.E.
Wright, Sec.-Lt. H. G., 3 N.F.Am.

The Fallen

England, Lt. E. W., K.O.Y.L.I.
Forbes, Lt. J. S., R.G.A.
Hutton, Pte. J. H., Northd. Fus.
Rishworth, K., R.A.F.
Stewart, Sec.-Lt. G., West Riding
Watson, Lt. J. C., Middlesex Rgt

Honours

Bilham, Capt. and Adj. D. G. R. M.C.
Jarman, Ft.-Lt. R., D.S.C.
Laverack, Capt. E., mentioned in despatches
Stephenson, Sap. R., M.M.

ENGLAND, E. W.
Lieutenant King's Own Yorkshire Light Infantry
Killed in action September 27th 1916
Hymers College

FORBES, J. S.
Lieutenant Royal Garrison Artillery
Hymers College

HUTTON, J. H.
Private 12/13th Northumberland Fusiliers
Wounded May 27th 1918 died in hospital at Bar-le-Duc June 6th 1918
Hymers College

RISHWORTH, K.
Royal Air Force
Hymers College

STEWART, GEORGE
2nd Lieutenant Duke of Wellington's West Riding Regiment
Killed in action in France April 10th 1918
Hymers College

WATSON, J. C.
Lieutenant Middlesex Regiment
Reported wounded and missing October 4th 1917
Hymers College

ILKLEY

Members who Joined the Forces

Ambler, Dvr. W., A.S.C. (M.T.)
Armistead, Capt. T. E., West Yks.
Atkinson, Pte. J., West Riding
Atkinson, Pte. W., A.S.C.
Atkinson, Pte. A. H., East Yorks.
Barnes, Pte. J., West Riding
Barnes, A.
Barnes, Sgt. E., 18 Hussars
Barwick, Gnr. T., R.F.A.
Bates, Lt. N., K.O.Y.L.I., attached King's African Rifles
Bates, Lt. R. S., 144 Reg. Ind. Ay.
Bell, Staff-Sgt. Farr. J., R.F.A.
Blagg, Gnr. J., Canadian F.A.
Boden, Pte. G. E., Australian Inf.
Bower, Gnr. W., R.F.A.
Bradley, Lt. W., R.A.F.
Broomhead, Gnr. J., R.F.A.
Brown, Dvr. H., A.S.C.
Brown, R.-Sgt.-Major W., R.F.A.
Burke, Pte. W., West Riding
Burns, Sgt.-Major P. C., A.S.C.
Clarkson, Pte. W., West Riding
Clay, Lt. A. B., R.A.F.
Collyer, Pte. A., West Riding
Cooper, Lt. A., M.G.C.
Cowbrough, L.-Cpl. S., West Yks.
Crowther, Sap. H., R.E.
Dacre, Lt. B., West Riding
Dawson, Lt. H., R.F.A.
Dean, Lt. R., West Riding
Dean, Dvr. C., R.F.A.
Dennison, Major P. B., A.O.C.
Dickinson, Bd. G., R.F.A.
Earnshaw, Bd. G. H., R.G.A.
Eaton, Pte. H., West Riding
Ellwood, Sgt J., West Riding
English, Capt. S. S., Leicester Rg.
Ettenfield, Pte. W., Nrthd. Fus.
Fisher, Pte. F., West Riding
Fisher, Sgt. J. W., West Riding
Forster, Lt. C. W., R.F.A.
Fox, Gnr. J., M.G.C.
Gaines, Sgt.-Maj. S., R.F.A.
Gallagher, L.-Cpl. F., West Rdg.
Garside, Gnr. R., R.F.A.
Geenty, Shoe.-Smith G., R. Fus.
Giles, Sgt. E., West Yorks.
Godby, Pte. H., A.P.C.
Green, Pte. V., A.S.C. (M.T.)
Hampshire, Sec.-Lt. E., R.F.A.
Hanson, Pte. W., Nrthd. Fus.
Hardisty, Pte. R., West Riding
Hargreaves, Cpl. W., A.O.C.
Harrison, Sgt. E. C. D., Scot. Hse.
Hastings, Sec.-Lt. E. B., R.F.A.
Hebblewhite, Dvr. W., R.F.A.
Higham, Pte. A., Canadian Inf.
Hobson, Gnr. A., R.F.A.
Holmes, Bd. W., R.G.A.
Holmes, A.B. E., R.N.A.S.
Holmes, Pte. A., West Riding
Holroyd, Lt. L., East Yorks.
Horner, Dvr. E., R.F.A.
Hudson, Gnr. E., R.F.A.
Ingham, Sgt. J., Australian Inf.
Keenan, Dvr. J., R.F.A.
King, L.-Cpl. J. A., Liverpool Scot.
Lambert, Pte. H. B., West Riding
Lambert, Dvr. L., R.F.A.
Lambert, Pte. J., West Riding
Lawson, Sap. W., R.E.
Lee, Lt. A. H., West Riding
Lister, Air Mech. C., R.A.F.
Locke, Lt. G. W., R.F.A.
Longfield, Capt. J. N., R.A.F.
Lund, Pte. J., West Riding
Matthews, Pte. H., West Yorks.
Maufe, Capt. F. W. B., R.F.A.
Middlebrook, Dvr. J., A.S.C. (M.T.)
Moore, Sec.-Lt. J. G., R.F.A.
Muller, Lt. N., West Yorks.
New, Gnr. F., R.F.A.
Nunns, Cpl.-Wheeler A., R.F.A.
O'Shea, Sap. P., R.E.
Peacock, Sgt. T., R.F.A.
Peacock, Sgt. H., R.F.A.
Pennock, Dvr. G., A.S.C. (M.T.)
Pennock, Dvr. R., A.S.C. (M.T.)
Petrie, Major P. C., R.F.A.
Petrie, Capt. F. E., Royal Fus.
Phillips, Pte. R., Canadian Inf.
Pinder, Dvr. R., R.F.A.
Pocklington, Dvr. W., R.F.A.
Rabagliati, Lt.-Col. E., R.A.F.
Rayner, Staff-Sgt.-Farr. S., Yorks. Hussars

ILKLEY—continued

Members who Joined the Forces—continued

RAYNER, Lt. W., R.F.A.
READSHAW, Bd. A., R.F.A.
RHODES, Lt. J. R., R.F.A.
ROBINSON, Sgt. F., R.A.M.C.
ROBINSON, Pte. R., West Riding
ROTHERAY, Major E., R.F.A.
SCARGILL, Capt. H. B., R.A.M.C.
SCOTT, Dvr. C., A.S.C. (M.T.)
SCOTT, Dvr. H., A.S.C. (M.T.)
SHARP, Capt. R., Lancashire Fus.
SHAW, Sap. E., Australian R.E.
SMITH, Sec.-Lt. G. M., R.F.A.
STONES, Pte. W., West Riding
STOTT, Pte. H., West Riding
SUTCLIFFE, Pte. G., R.A.M.C.
SWALES, Bomb. W. A., R.F.A.
THIRKILL, Shg.-Smith W., R.F.A.
THOMPSON, Lt. J. N., R.F.A.
THOMSON, D., Royal Fus.
THORNTON, Gnr. W., R.F.A.
THORPE, Lt. R., R.F.A.
THWAITES, Pte. E., K.R.R.
WALKER, Capt. P. H. C., R.F.A.
WILKINSON, Capt. E., West Yorks.
WRAITH, Lt. H D., West Riding

The Fallen

ARMISTEAD, Capt. T. E., M.C. West Yorks.
ATKINSON, Pte. J., West Riding
BARNES, Sgt. E., 18 Hussars
BLAGG, Cpl. J., Canadian F.A.
BRADLEY, Lt. W., R.A.F.
DACRE, Lt. B., West Riding
DAWSON, Lt. H., R.F.A.
DEAN, Lt. R., D.C.M.,West Riding
EARNSHAW, Bd. G. H., R.G.A.
FISHER, Pte. F., West Riding
GALLAGHER, L.-Cpl. F., West Rdg.
GREEN, Pte. V., A.S.C. (M.T.)
HARDISTY, Pte R., West Riding
HIGHAM, Pte. A., Canadian Inf.
HOLROYD, Lt. L., East Yorks.
KING, L.-Cpl. J. A., Liverpool Scot.
LEE, Lt. A. H., West Riding
LUND, Pte. J., West Riding
MULLER, Lt. N., West Yorks.
NUNNS, Cpl.-Wheeler A., R.F.A.
O'SHEA, Sap. P., R.E.
PHILLIPS, Pte. R., Canadian Inf.
ROBINSON, Sgt. F., R.A.M.C.
SMITH, Sec.-Lt. G. M., M.C., R.F.A.
THIRKILL, Shg.-Smith W., R.F.A.
THWAITES, Pte. E., K.R.R.
WILKINSON, Capt. E., M.C., W.Y.

Honours

ARMISTEAD, T. E., M.C.
CLARKSON, W., D.C.M.
DEAN, R., D.C.M.
DENNISON, P. B., M.C.
ENGLISH, S. S., mentioned in despatches
GAINES, S., M.M.
HEBBLEWHITE, W., M.M.
MAUFE, F. W. B., M.C. and bar, mentioned in despatches
PETRIE, P. C., D.S O., M.C. mentioned in despatches (2)
RABAGLIATI, E., M.C., mentioned in despatches
RHODES, J. R., D.C.M.
SHARP, R., mentioned in despatches
SMITH, G. M., M.C.
WALKER, P. H. C., M.C. and bar mentioned in despatches
WILKINSON, E., M.C. and bar mentioned in despatches

ARMISTEAD, T. E., M.C.
Captain 6th West Yorkshire Regiment
Killed May 3rd 1917
Ilkley R.F.C.

ATKINSON, JOHN
Private West Riding Regiment
Wounded November 20th, died at Rouen December 21st 1917
Ilkley R.F.C.

BLAGG, J.
Corporal Shoeing-smith Royal Canadian Horse Artillery
Died of wounds in France August 10th 1919
Ilkley R.F.C

BRADLEY, W. R.
Lieutenant and Adjutant Royal Air Force
Died of malaria fever in Salonica June 29th 1918
Ilkley R.F.C.

DACRE, BRIAN
Captain Duke of Wellington's West Riding Regiment
Killed October 12th 1918
Ilkley R.F.C.

DEAN, ARTHUR REGINALD, D.C.M.
2nd Lieutenant
Killed in action July 3rd 1917
Ilkley R.F.C.

EARNSHAW, GEORGE HENRY
Bombardier 323rd Siege Battery Royal Garrison Artillery
Killed April 18th 1918
Ilkley R.F.C.

FISHER, FRED
Private 9th Duke of Wellington's West Riding Regiment
Killed May 5th 1916
Ilkley R.F.C.

GALLAGHER, FRED
Lance-Corporal 1/6th Duke of Wellington's West Riding Regiment
Killed December 19th 1915
Ilkley R.F.C.

HIGHAM, ARTHUR SAMUEL
Private 43rd Scottish Canadians
Killed October 4th 1916
Ilkley R.F.C.

HOLROYD, LISTER
Captain 7th East Yorkshire Regiment
Wounded on the Somme September 1st, died at Etretat September 12th
1916
Ilkley R.F.C.

LEE, ARTHUR BASIL
2nd Lieutenant 5th West Yorkshire Regiment
Killed July 2nd 1916
Ilkley R.F.C.

LUND, J. A.
Private 9th Duke of Wellington's West Riding Regiment
Died in France February 21st 1919
Ilkley R F.C.

NUNNS, WILLIAM ARTHUR
Corporal-Wheeler 4th West Riding Brigade Royal Field Artillery
Died in hospital at Boulogne September 17th 1915
Ilkley R.F.C

SMITH, GODFREY MICHAEL
2nd Lieutenant 51st Division Royal Field Artillery
Died of wounds October 28th 1918
Ilkley R.F.C.

SMITH, W.
Gunner Royal Field Artillery
Killed in action
Ilkley R.F.C.

THIRKELL, WALTER
Shoeing-Smith 4th West Riding Howitzer Brigade 11th Battery Royal Field Artillery
Died from pneumonia March 3rd 1919 while on demobilisation furlough
Ilkley R.F.C.

THWAITES, EDWARD
Private 2/6th Duke of Wellington's West Riding Regiment
Killed in action in Bourlon Wood November 27th 1917
Ilkley R.F.C.

WILKINSON, ERIC FITZWATER
Captain 1/8th West Yorkshire Regiment
Killed in action October 9th 1917
Ilkley R.F.C.

ILKLEY GRAMMAR SCHOOL

Members who Joined the Forces

AKEROYD, Wire.-Oper. G. M., Mercantile Marine
ATKINSON, Lt. J. C., R.E.
BARTLE, Pte. J. A., L. North Lanc.
BOX, Lt. C. A., R.A.F.
BOX, Cdt. A. D., R.A.F.
BREFFIT, Pte. S. W., Canadians
BROWNLOW, Capt. G. F. S., Manch.
BURNS, Sec.-Lt. J. F., M.M.G.C.
CAMPBELL, Seaman W., R.N.
CAWDRY, Sub-Lt. C. J., R.N.
COBBY, Staff-Capt. W. M., R.G.A.
CORNWELL, Pte. E. H., Nth. Staffs.
DOVE, Gnr. F. R., R.F.A.
EVANS, Lt. W. A., R.A.F.
GEENTY, Pte. J., R.A.F.
GLEDHILL, Lt. A. D., R.A.F.
GRAHAM, Lt. H., R.A.F.
HARDAKER, C.
HEWITT, Pte. R., Leicester Regt.
HOPE, Cdt. E. C., Canadian R.A.F.
HOUSEMAN, Pte. H., K.O.Y.L.I.
HUGHES, Lt. J., R.A.F.
JOHNSON, Cpl. J. A., West Riding
LABATT, Sec.-Lt. W. H.E., R.A.F.
LICKFOLD, Lt. E. R, R.A.F.
LUPTON, Lt. G. V., A.S.C.
MAJOR, Midshipman S. E , R.N.
MOISLEY, Pte. H., Devon Regt.
MOXON, Pte. A., Royal Marines
MOXON, Seaman T., R.N.
MOXON, Lt. P., R.F.A.
MUSGRAVE, K. W., Leeds O.T.C.
PARRATT, Cpl. H. S., Leicester Rgt.
RUSSELL, Pte. C. L., A.S.C.
SELLERS, Gnr. G., H.A.C.
SMITH, Pte. H., D.L.I.
SYKES, Lt. E., R.A.F.
TODD, Sec.-Lt. N. S., R.A.F.
TUNNICLIFFE, Lt. W. A. M., R.G.A.
TWEED, Cdt. A. R. M., Camb. Uni. O.T.C.
WILKINSON, Pte. B. I., A.S.C.
WHITE, Lt. J. W., R.A.F.

Honours

ATKINSON, Lt. J. C., M.C.
BURNS, Sec.-Lt. J. F., M.C.

COBBY, Staff-Capt. W. M., M.C.

LEEDS GRAMMAR SCHOOL

Members who Joined the Forces

ALLAN, W. H., 2 W.R., R.A.M.C.
BARRETT, A., Grenadier Guards
BENTON, G. C., 1 W.R., R.F.A.
BLACKBURN, Sec.-Lt. J. T., R.F.A.
BOLTON, Lt. R. L., West Yorks.
BRECKIN, W., Artists' Rifles
BROADBENT, Sec.-Lt. C. S., Tanks
BUCK, Sec.-Lt. J. M., Worcester R.
CAMPBELL, Lt. W. A., R.F.C.
CHAPPLE, Surg.-Prob. K. R., R.N.V.R.
CLARKE, Sec.-Lt. A. L., R.F.A.
CROSSLAND, P., West Yorks.
CROSSLEY, Sec.-Lt. J. V., R.G.A.
DALBY, Capt. A. A., West Yorks.
FERRO, Sec.-Lt. R. T., R.F.A.
FRICKER, Lt. E., West Yorks.
GLEDHILL, L.-Cpl. N., Staffs. Yeo.
HILDITCH, Sec.-Lt. S., K.O.Y.L.I.
HININGS, Sec.-Lt. C. I., East Yks.
HODGSON, Sec.-Lt. A. B., R.G.A.
HODGSON, D. V., Cadet Sch. R.F.C.
HOGGETT, F. N., R.E.
HOLLIS, Sec.-Lt. A. M., Gren. Gds.
HORNER, Sec.-Lt. K. C., R.F.C.
LAUGHTON, Sec.-Lt. G., Nrthd. F.
LYON, Sec.-Lt. D. H., West Riding
McGUIRE, G. T. D., Leeds O.T.C.
SANDERSON, Sec.-Lt. R. W., E. Sur.
STEWART, Ft.-Lt. J. D. M., R.F.C.
STORRS, Sec.-Lt. H. H., R.F.C.
WALTON, V., R.F.A.
WHITAKER, Lt. G. G., Y. & L.
WHITFIELD, Sec.-Lt. R. C., Y. & L.
WILLANS, Sec.-Lt. G. R., Lancs. F.
WILSON, Sec.-Lt. A., Nrthd. Fus.
WOOD, Sec.-Lt. E., O.C.B.
WRIGHT, Sec.-Lt. H. J., Sandhurst
WYNNE-EDWARDS, Capt. R. M., Royal Welsh Fus.

The Fallen

BARRETT, A., Grenadier Guards
BENTON, G. C., 1 W.R., R.F.A.
CAMPBELL, Lt. W. A., R.F.C.
HORNER, Sec.-Lt. K. C., R.F.C.
LAUGHTON, Sec.-Lt. G., Nrthd. F.
LYON, Sec.-Lt. D. H., West Riding
WILLANS, Sec.-Lt. G. R., Lancs. F.

Honours

FRICKER, Lt. E., M.C.
WYNNE-EDWARDS, Capt. R. M., D.S.O., M.C. and bar, mentioned in despatches

BARRETT, ALEC
Grenadier Guards
July 22nd 1917
Leeds Grammar School ·

BENTON, GEORGE CYRIL
1st West Riding R.F.A.
June 10th 1916
Leeds Grammar School

HORNER, KARL CHRISTIAN
2nd Lieutenant Royal Air Force
April 4th 1917
Leeds Grammar School

LAUGHTON, GEOFFREY
2nd Lieutenant Northumberland Fusiliers
Leeds Grammar School

LYON, DONALD HALLIDAY
2nd Lieutenant West Riding Regiment
September 20th 1917
Leeds Grammar School

LEEDS RIFLES
(7th and 8th West Yorks. Regt.)

ALL THE PLAYERS WERE MOBILISED ON 4TH AUGUST 1914

THE FALLEN

FEAR, R.S.M. W., 8 West Yorks.
GILL, Cpl. H., 2/8 West Yorks.
GOODSON, Sec.-Lt. G., 8 West Yorks. and Australian Force
GREEN, L.-Cpl. W. C., 8 West Yorks. and Navy
HARTNELL, Lt. C., 8 West Yorks.

LUPTON, Capt. M., 7 West Yorks.
MIDGLEY, Rfn. E.
MYERS, C.S.M. D. F., 8 West Yks.
PERRY, C.S.M. R., 8 West Yorks.
POTTS, Sec.-Lt. W. E., 2/8 W.Y.
SHAW, Cpl. J. H., 8 West Yorks.
SIMON, Sgt. C. R., 7 West Yorks.

HONOURS

8 Batt. P.W.O. West Yorks. Rgt. Croix de Guerre
ASHCROFT, Pte. M., M.M.
BALDWIN, Capt. F. J., M.C.
BROOKE, Major W. H., D.S.O.
CARNES, Sec.-Lt. C., M.C.

FEAR, R.S.M. W., M.C.
GLAZEBROOK, Lt., M.C.
LONGBOTTOM, Major T., D.S.O.
POTTS, Sec.-Lt. W. E., M.M.
SPENCE, C.S.M. C., D.C.M.

FEAR, W.
Regimental-Sergeant-Major 8th West Yorkshire Regiment (Leeds Rifles)
Killed in action 1916
Leeds Rifles R.F.C.

GILL, H.
Corporal 8th West Yorkshire Regiment (Leeds Rifles)
Killed in action 1917
Leeds Rifles R.F.C.

GOODSON, A. G.
2nd Lieutenant 8th West Yorkshire Regiment (Leeds Rifles) and
Australian Force
Killed in action August 4th 1916
Leeds Rifles R.F.C.

GREEN, W. C.
Lance-Corporal 8th West Yorkshire Regiment, Leeds Rifles, and Navy
Killed in action February 29th 1916 on the "Alcantara" in
her fight with the raider "Grieff." Both vessels sank
Leeds Rifles R.F.C.

HARTNELL, C.
Lieutenant 8th West Yorkshire Regiment (Leeds Rifles)
Killed in action June 1915
Leeds Rifles R.F.C.

LUPTON, M.
Captain 7th West Yorkshire Regiment (Leeds Rifles)
Killed in action June 19th 1915
Leeds Rifles R.F.C.

MYERS, D. F.
Company-Sergeant Major 8th West Yorkshire Regiment (Leeds Rifles)
Killed in action August 1915
Leeds Rifles R.F.C.

PERRY, R.
Company-Sergeant-Major 8th West Yorkshire Regiment (Leeds Rifles)
Killed in action 1916
Leeds Rifles R.F.C.

POTTS, WILLIAM EDGAR, M.M.
2nd Lieutenant 5th West Yorkshire Regiment
Missing, believed killed April 13th 1918
Leeds Grammar School and Leeds Rifles R.F.C.

SHAW, J. H.
Corporal 8th West Yorkshire Regiment (Leeds Rifles)
Killed in action June 1915
Leeds Rifles R.F.C.

SIMON, C. R.
Sergeant 7th West Yorkshire Regiment (Leeds Rifles)
Killed in action May 1915
Leeds Rifles R.F.C.

LEEDS YARNBURY

Members who Joined the Forces

ALLEN, Lt. J., West Riding Regt.
ARMITAGE, Sgt. H., West Yorks.
BARKER, L.-Cpl. G., M.G.C.
BARKER, Lt. E., R.F.A.
BELLIS, Lt. R., West Yorks.
BOOTH, Capt. A. E., Indian Army
BOOTH, Capt. G. L., 7 West Yorks.
BOSTON, Sec.-Lt. R., R.H.A.
BOSTON, Lt. E., R.G.A.
BOTTOMLEY, Capt. D., A.S.C.
BOTTOMLEY, Sgt. N., R.F.A.
BRIGGS, Pte. C., London Scottish
BRIGGS, Cpl. J., R.F.A.
CHADWICK, Sec.-Lt. C., West Yks.
COBB, Lt. M. D., A.I.F.
COBB, Sgt. G., R.A.M.C.
CORDINGLEY, R.S.M. A., R.A.M.C.
FLESHER, Capt. H., R.E.
FLETCHER, Dvr. F., R.F.A.
FLETCHER, Pte. J., R.A.M.C.
FRAPE, Staff-Sgt. H., Gym. Staff
GARNETT, A.M. 1. P., R.A.F.
GLEDHILL, Lt. M., R.A.F.
GREEN, Sgt. R., West Yorks.
HELLEWELL, Pte. J., R.A.M.C.
HELLEWELL, Cpl. G., R.A.F.
JILBERT, Bmd. J., R.G.A.
LAWTON, Capt. H., West Yorks.
LEGG, Major H., A.S.C.
LILLIE, Pte. R., West Yorks.
LINDLEY, C.Q.M.S. F., A.S.C.
LINDLEY, Lt. B., London Regt.
MILLER, Lt. J. W., York & Lancs.
MILLS, Shoeingsmith W., Yorks. H.
MOTLEY, Lt. P., 7 West Yorks.
MOULD, Bmd. J., R.F.A.
NEVITT, Capt. G., West Yorks.
RAWLINS, Capt. C. B., R.F.A.
RICHARDSON, Sec.-Lt. A. V., West Riding Regt.
ROBINSON, Lt. M., West Yorks.
SHAW, Lt. E., Argyle & Sutherd. H.
SHEARD, Lt. W. H., Welsh Regt.
SIMPSON, Capt. J., A.S.C.
SPINK, A.M. 1 W. H., R.A.F.
THOMPSON, Lt. G., R.E.
WESTMORELAND, Sap. G., R.E.
WHITWORTH, Sgt. C., M.G.C.
WILCHER, Capt. B. L., 17 West Yk.
WILSON, Sgt. JACK, Canadians
WOOD, Cpl. L. A., R.F.A.

The Fallen

BARRAND, S.
BENTON, G.
BENTON, J.
BRIGGS, R. C.
BRIGGS, O.
BROOK, C.
FLESHER, A.
HURTLEY, T.
LILLIE, F.
MCMULLEN, E. N.
MELLOR, A.
NEVITT, G.
RAYNER, H.
WILCHER, H.

Honours

BOOTH, Capt. G. L., 7 West Yorks. M.C.
FLESHER, Capt. H., R.E., M.C.
LAWTON, Capt. H., West Yorks. M.C.
RAWLINS, Lt. C. B., R.F.A., M.C.

BARRAND, SYDNEY
Lieutenant 1st King's Royal Rifle Corps
Twice wounded
Killed August 14th 1918
Leeds Yarnbury R.F.C.

BRIGGS, ORRIE
Captain 8th York and Lancaster Regiment
Killed November 4th 1918
Leeds Yarnbury R.F.C.

LILLIE, F.
2nd Lieutenant 11th King's Own Yorkshire Light Infantry
Killed December 18th 1916
Leeds Yarnbury R.F.C.

RAYNER, HAROLD
2nd Lieutenant East Yorkshire Regiment
Reported missing September 4th 1918
Leeds Yarnbury R.F.C.

WILCHER, HAROLD
2nd Lieutenant 3rd King's Own Yorkshire Light Infantry
Died of wounds July 5th received in action July 1st 1916
Leeds Yarnbury R.F.C.

OTLEY

MEMBERS WHO JOINED THE FORCES

ATKINSON, Dvr. W., 4 W.R.,R.F.A.
BARKER, Capt. N., R.E.
BARKER, Sgt. S., R.E.
BARKER, Lt. F., 4 W.R., R.F.A.
BARRETT, L.-Cpl. T., R.E.
BARTLE, Pte. J. A., L. North Lanc.
BOOTH, Pte. H., R.A.M.C.
BROTHERTON, Cpl. W., 4 East Yks.
BROTHERTON, Sgt. T., 4 W.R., R.F.A.
BROWN, Cpl. A., West Yorks.
BROWN, Cpl. H., A.S.C.
BROWN, Pte. E., 1/4 West Riding
BRUMFITT, Pte. H., 4 W.R., R.F.A.
BRUMFITT, Pte. E., 4 W R., R.F.A.
CAIRNS, Bd. H., 4 W.R., R.F.A.
CROWE, Bd. G., 4 W.R., R.F.A.
CROWE, Sgt. S. E., R.A.M.C.
CROWE, Sec.-Lt. J. E., West Yks.
DARNBOROUGH, Bd. H., 4 W.R., R.F.A.
DUNCAN, Lt.-Col., 4 W.R., R.F.A.
DUNCAN, Major H. S., 4 W.R., R.F.A.
DUNCAN, Capt. H., 4 W.R., R.F.A.
ELLIOT, Staff-Sgt. D. A., R.G.A.
GEENTY, Air-Mech. J., R.A.F.
HALSTEAD, Pte. F., 49 Gordon H.
HELLEWELL, Sec.-Lt. S., West Yk.
HOLGATE, Gnr. H., 4 W.R., R.F.A.
HOLGATE, Gnr. T., 4 W.R., R.F.A.
HYMAS, Cpl. F., 4 W.R., R.F.A.
JANES, Dvr. J., 4 W.R., R.F.A.
KIDD, Major V., West Riding
LAMBERT, Pte. G., East Yorks.
LAWSON, Cpl. J., 4 W.R., R.F.A.
LOCKWOOD, Sec.-Lt. A., R.G.A.
MASON, Lt. D. C., 4 W.R., R.F.A.
MASON, Pte. B., 4 West Riding
MOXON, A.B. Seaman T., R.N.
NORFOLK, Pte. E., 1/4 West Rdg.
OTHIC, Sgt. W., West Riding
PRESTON, Pte. W., 1/9 West Rdg.
RALPH, Sec.-Lt. H., R.E.
ROBINSON, Sgt. J., West Riding
STEVENSON, Staff-Sgt. H. F., 245 Brigade R.F.A.
TODD, Bd. H., 4 W.R., R.F.A.
TONKS, Lt.
WALKER, Cdt. J., 4 W.R., R.F.A.
WALKER, Pte. H., R.A.M.C.
WARBURTON, Capt. J. W., K.O.Y.L.I.
WARBURTON, Petty-Off. H., R.N.
WILKINSON, Air-Mech. E., R.A.F.
WILLIS, Bd. J., 4 W.R., R.F.A.
WINTERBURN, Lt. J., R.G.A.
WISE, Sgt. A., 245 Brigade R.F.A.
WRIGHT, Artificer H., R.N.A.S.

THE FALLEN

ELLIOT, Staff-Sgt. D. A., R.G.A.
HYMAS, Cpl. F., 4 W.R., R.F.A.
KIDD, Major V., West Riding
LOCKWOOD, Sec.-Lt. A., R.G.A.
PRESTON, Pte. W., 1/9 West Rdg.
STEVENSON, Staff-Sgt. H. F., 245 Brigade R.F.A.
TODD, Bd. H., 4 W.R., R.F.A.
WISE, Sgt. A., 245 Brigade R.F.A.

HONOURS

BARKER, Capt. N., O.B.E.
BROTHERTON, Sgt. T., twice mentioned in despatches
CROWE, Bd. G., M.M.
DUNCAN, Lt.-Col., D.S.O. and two bars
DUNCAN, Major H. S., M.C.
OTHIC, Sgt. W., Croix de Guerre, M.M., 1914 Star
WISE, Sgt. A., M.M.

ELLIOTT, DOUGLAS A.
Staff-Sergeant Army Ordnance Corps, Royal Garrison Artillery
Killed March 21st 1918
Otley R.F.C.

HYMAS, S. S.
Corporal 240th West Riding Brigade Royal Field Artillery (T.F.)
Killed near Cambrai October 11th 1918
Otley R.F.C.

KIDD, VIVIAN, M.C.
Major Duke of Wellington's West Riding Regiment
Killed in action March 1917
Otley and Headingley R.F.C.

LOCKWOOD A.
2nd Lieutenant Royal Field Artillery
Killed in action March 28th 1917
Otley R.F.C.

PRESTON, WOOD
Private Royal Field Artillery
Killed in action in France
Otley R.F.C.

STEPHENSON, H. F.
Staff-Sergeant Royal Field Artillery
Died of wounds March 27th 1918
Otley R.F.C

TODD, H.
Bombardier Royal Field Artillery
Died of wounds
Otley R.F.C.

WISE, ARTHUR, M.M.
Sergeant 4th West Riding Brigade Royal Field Artillery
Killed in action at Passchendaele November 3rd 1917
Otley R.F.C.

POCKLINGTON SCHOOL

Members who Joined the Forces

ALLDRED, Sec.-Lt. R. A., 3 L.N.L.
ALLDRED, Sec.-Lt. S. D., R.F.A.
ATKINSON, Sec.-Lt. J. F. V., R.A.F.
BARCLAY, Cdt. F. J. S., R.A.F.
BRYERS, Capt. G. F., R.A.F.
BURBIDGE, Sec.-Lt. J. C., Rfl. Bgd.
COCKBURN, Pte. P. C., R.E.
COLLINGTON, Sec.-Lt. W. A. A., Gloucester Regt.
COULSON, Sec.-Lt. A. T., Yks. Hus.
COULSON, Sec.-Lt. C. R., R.A.F.
GIBSON, Rfn. W. N., Rifle Bgd.
GOODLASS, Sec.-Lt. C. W., 3 Y.R
GRAY-JARVIS, Pte. J., Artist Rifles O.T.C.
HIGHMORE, Sec.-Lt. G. W., 3 Y.R.
LANYON, Sec.-Lt. E. C., K.S.L.I.
LESLIE, Capt. W. L., Sth. Shrops.
LOCKERBIE, Sec.-Lt. H. L., R.S.F.
MALLINSON, Pte. C. A., West Yks.
MILLAR, Pte. D. W., Inns Ct. O.T.C.
MORRIS, Sec.-Lt. B. A., Royal Scts.
PENNINGTON, Lt. G. A., R.A.F.
PETTER, Sec.-Lt. N., 6 D.L.I.
ROBINSON, Sec.-Lt. H., 91 Punjabis
SAMPSON, Capt. A. C., 25 Lon. Rfls.
STRONG, Sec.-Lt. J. R., D.Crn.L.I.
STUBBS, Pte. L. A., West Yorks.
WADESON, Sec.-Lt. E Y., 3 L.N.L.
WOOD, Lt. G. C., R.F.A.

The Fallen

LOCKERBIE, Sec.-Lt. H. L., Royal Scots Fusiliers
WADESON, Sec.-Lt. E. Y., 3 Loyal North Lancs.

Honours

PENNINGTON, Lt. G. A., Croce di Guerra (Italy)
SAMPSON, Capt. A. C., M.C. and bar
WOOD, Lt. G. C., M.C.

PUDSEY

Members who Joined the Forces

CHAPMAN, Pte. E., West Riding
CHAPMAN, Gnr. W., R.F.A.
CROWTHER, Sgt. T., West Yorks.
ELLIS, Cpl. J., 1 East Yorks.
HELLOWELL, Capt. J. W., Yks. R.
HUGGAN, Lt. GEORGE
HYLAND, Cpl. C., 2 Life Guards
HYLAND, Sec.-Lt. W , 8 West Yks.
HYLAND, Sec.-Lt. J. L., 4 West Rd.
JUBB, Pte. C , M.G C.
KENWORTHY, Capt. W., R.A.M.Ç.
MANN, C.Q.M.S. G. W., West Yks.
McCAULEY, Capt. C. E., Legion of Frontiersmen
MILNER, Dvr. H , A.S.C.
NAYLOR, Capt. Rev. A. T. A., C.F.
RHODES, Cpl. W. H. R.M.L.I.
SMITH, Pte. A. E., West Yorks.
THORPE, Capt. F., M.G.C.
TIDSWELL, Pte. J., Army Cyc. C
TURNER, Lt. NORMAN, 12 West Yk.
VARLEY, Cpl. F., West Yorks.
WALKER, Sec.-Lt. M., West Yorks.
WALKER, Pte. W., Army Cyc. C
WALKER, Pte. E., Army Cyc. C.
WEBSTER, Gnr. J. W , R.G.A.
WEBSTER, Gnr. J., R.G.A.
WOOD, Pte. C., Royal Welsh Fus.

The Fallen

TURNER, Lt. NORMAN, 12 West Yorks.

BARRETT, LEONARD
Lance-Corporal 21st King's Royal Rifle Corps
Killed in action on the Somme, France, September 15th 1916
Pudsey R.F.C.

HORTON, REV. PAUL F.
Lance-Corporal
Killed in France September 28th 1917
Pudsey R.F.C.

TURNER, H. NORMAN
Lieutenant 15th West Yorkshire Regiment
Killed near Montauban July 14th 1916
Pudsey R.F.C.

RIPON GRAMMAR SCHOOL

Members who Joined the Forces

Bland, Ft.-Sub-Lt. D., R.N.A.S.
Cartwright, Lt. S. F., R.F.A.
Dove, Lt. J. D., R.G.A.
Ducksbury, Sec.-Lt. H. A., EastY.
Flesher, Sec.-Lt. A. F., 6 R. War.
Garrod, Capt. W. E., West Yorks.
George, Sec.-Lt. W. L., A.S.C.
Goldsworthy, Sec.-Lt. G. W., West Riding
Hamilton, Lt. A. S., 15 West Yks.
Hamilton, Capt. J. S., 2/7 West Y.
Hamilton, Sec.-Lt. T., 7 West Yk.
Hartley, B., R.N.R.
Headlam, Lt. J, R.A.F.
Ireland, Sec.-Lt. J. B., Black Watch
Jameson, Lt. J. L., 5 West Yorks.
Jameson, Lt. H., R.F.A.
Kingdon, Bd. W. L., 3 H.A.C.
Lee, Sec.-Lt. R. W., West Riding
Marston, Sec.-Lt. P. J., D.L.I.
Morton, J. S., K.R.R.
Morton, F., Yorks. Hussars
Nicholas, J. N., C.S. Rifles
North, Lt. E., Q.O. Yorks. Drgs.
North, Lt. W. L., O.C.B.
Pickard, Lt. R. L., R.F.A.
Read, J. W., R.N.A.S.
Richardson, A. M., R.F.C.
Southern, Sec.-Lt. V. G., 5 West Yorks.
Spence, A. W., R.N.A.S. (P.F.O.)
Surry, Gnr. B. S., R.G.A.
Taylor, E., R.F.C.
Thirlway, Lt. M. H., 11 Y. & L.
Thirlway, R., Training Reserve
Thompson, Lt. S., R.F.A.
Tilston, Lt. E., 19 Royal Fus.
Wells, W., 2 D.L.I.
Wells, Lt. W. N., 1 West Yorks.
Wells, Lt. A. S., Nrthd. Fus.
Wilcox, Sec.-Lt. H., 5 West Yks.

The Fallen

Cartwright, Lt. S. F., R.F.A.
Flesher, Sec.-Lt. A. F., 6 R. War.
Hamilton, Sec.-Lt. T., 7 West Yk.
Headlam, Lt. J., R.A.F.
Jameson, Lt. J. L., M.C., 5 West. Y.
Marston, Sec.-Lt. P. J., D.L.I.
Tilston, Lt. E., 19 Royal Fus.
Wells, Lt. A. S., Nrthd. Fus.

Honours

Garrod, Capt. W. E., M.C. and bar
Goldsworthy, Sec.-Lt. G. W., M.C.
Hamilton, Capt. J. S., D.S.O.
Hamilton, Lt. Tom, M.B.E.
Hartley, B., D.S.C.
Jameson, J. L., M.C.
Jameson, Lt. H., M.C. and bar
Southern, Sec.-Lt. V. G., M.C., mentioned in despatches
Wells, W., M.M.

ROYAL SCOTS GREYS

THE FALLEN

GILLMORE, Pte., 1914
HURST, Pte., 1918, Somme (1914 Star)
MATHIESON, Sgt., March 1918 (promoted Lieut Bedford Regiment)
PATTERSON, Sgt., 1917, Arras (1914 Star)
ROMANIS, Pte., March 1918
WILSON, Pte., 1914, Ypres (1914 Star)

HONOURS

COOPER, Capt., Russian Order St. Stanilas, Belgian Cher-Order of Leopold, Belgian Croix de Guerre, 1914 Star
CRABBE, Lt., Russian Order St. Anne, M.C., 1914 Star, and promoted Brevet-Major. Mentioned in despatches
CRANSTON, Sgt., now Lt.-Col. M.G.C., D.S.O., Russian Cross St. George, 1914 Star. Mentioned in despatches
ELLIOTT, R.S.M., Belgian Croix de Guerre
GIBSON, Pte., now R.S.M. M.G.C., M.C.
JONES, Sgt., now Capt. Welsh Regiment, M.M., 1914 Star
McNAUGHTON, S.S.M., now Capt. Seaforth Highlanders, 1914 Star
MITCHELL, Sgt., now Lieut Cameron Highlanders, M.C., 1914 Star
MORGAN, Sgt., now Capt. York and Lancaster Regiment, M.C.
RAILTON, Sgt., now Capt. York and Lancaster Regiment, 1914 Star
READMAN, Capt., D.S.O. Mentioned in despatches
ROBINSON, Sgt., now Capt. Royal Horse Artillery, French Croix de Guerre, 1914 Star
SIMPSON, Sgt., now Capt. Liverpool Regiment, M.C., 1914 Star

PATTERSON, WILLIAM
Sergeant Royal Scots Greys
Killed in action near Arras April 11th 1917
Royal Scots Greys R.F.C.

WILSON, R.
Private Royal Scots Greys
Killed in action at Ypres November 1st 1914
Royal Scots Greys R.F.C.

SHEFFIELD

Members who Joined the Forces

Allen, Lt. B. G., 2 Sherwood
Allen, Lt. S., Ulster Vols.
Ashwin, Lt. H., R.E.
Atkinson, R., Y. & L.
Benson, Lt. B. J., R.F.A.
Benson, Lt. R. C., R.F.A.
Bingham, Lt.-Col. Sir A. E., R.E.
Blatherwick, Capt. R., R.A.F.
Brown, J. C.
Cole, Lt. K. L., Sheff. City Batt.
Colley, Major L. E., R.E.
Colver, Capt. H., 5 Y. & L.
Colver, Lt. E. W., R.E.
Dickinson, S. P.
Duplock, Lt. F M., Nigerian Regt.
Dust, Capt. F. W., R.F.A.
Dyson, Lt., Y. & L.
Ewbank, Rev. H., 1 Border Regt.
Farrant, Capt. M., R.F.A.
Firth, Lt.-Col. B. A. 4 Y. & L.
Fisher, Major J. M., York & Lanc.
Forsdike, Capt. A. W., R.F.A.
Fowler, Capt. G. W., R.F.A.
Fraser, Lt. J. N., Yorks. Drgs.
Ginn, H.
Grundy, G. L.
Gwynne, Lt. J. F., R.A.M.C.
Gwynne, Lt. O. P., Y. & L.
Haggie, Pte. J. D., Artists' Rifles
Henderson, Lt., Y. & L.
Henkel, Lt. W., West Yorks.
Hess, Capt. J. M. L., Y. & L.
Hewson, Lt. F. B., Y. & L.

Holmstrom, Pte. E., Artists' Rfls.
Howe, Lt. P., Y. & L.
Howson, Capt. H. G., R.F.A.
Jackson, Lt. J., York & Lancs.
Leslie, Capt. O. E. H., R.G.A.
Llewellyn, Lt. L. C., Monmths.
Lucas, Lt. W. H., Y. & L.
Ludlam, Major F., Yorks. Drgs.
Marsh, Capt. J. L., Y. & L.
Moulding, W.
Orr, Lt. H. J., R.N.
Osborn, Lt. E., Labour Corps
Paddock, Lt., R.F.A.
Parry, Lt. N. C., 3 West Yorks.
Paul, Capt. A. S., Queen's Bays
Richardson, Major J. W., Y. & L.
Ronksley, Lt. H., R.A.F.
Roberts, Lt. G. H., Y. & L.
Rutherford, Capt R. H., R.A.M.C
Sales, Lt. W. T., R.F.A.
Schweder, H. A.
Scott, Major E. I., R.E.
Spital, J. T., R.A.F.
Stainforth, Capt. R., Sher. Fstrs.
Turner, Lt.-Col. Dr., R.A.M.C.
Turner, A. W.
Wales, Major C. E., 3 West Yorks.
Walsh, A. C. M., R.A.
Weyer, Capt. A. O., R.E.
Willey, Major H., R.G.A.
Wilson, Capt. A. K., Y. & L.
Wilson, Lt.-Col. R. E., Y. & L.
Wortley, Capt. J. F., 4 Y. & L.

The Fallen

Cole, Lt. K. L., Y. & L.
Colver, Capt. H., Y. & L.
Colver, Lt. E. W., R.E.
Dust, Capt. F. W., R.F.A.
Dyson, Lt., Y. & L.
Ginn, H.
Gwynne, Lt. O. P., Y. & L

Gwynne, Lt. J. F., R.A.M.C.
Henderson, Lt., Y. & L.
Marsh, Capt. J. L., Y. & L.
Parry, Lt. N. C., West Yorks.
Richardson, Major J., Y. & L.
Roberts, Lt. G. H., K.O.L.Y.I.
Wortley, Capt. J. F., Y. & L.

Honours

Bingham, Lt.-Col. Sir A. E., Bart. O.B.E.
Fisher, Major J. M., D.S.O., M C
Fowler, Capt. G. N., M.C., Croix de Guerre
Henkel, Lt. W., M.C.
Howson, Capt. H., M.C. and Italian decoration
Leslie, Capt. O. E. H., M.C.

Ludlam, Major F., M.C.
Ronksley, Capt. H., M.C.
Scott, Major E. I., M.C.
Stainforth, Capt. R., M.C.
Turner, Lt.-Col. Dr., D.S.O.
Wales, Major C. E., M.C.
Willey, Major H., Croix de Guerre
Wilson, Major R. E., M.C. and bar

SHEFFIELD UNIVERSITY

Members who Joined the Forces

BATES, H. N.
BENNET, J.
BENSON, B. J.
BENSON, R. C.
BIDDULPH, M. A.
GORDON, E. R. A.
KEMP, G. S. L.
LUCAS, N. O.

PERCIVAL, J. L.
PERKIN, K.
ROBINSON, W.
SECKER, C.
SOMERSET, R. M.
TURNER, S.
WHITTAKER, H.

The Fallen

GORDON, E. R. A.
PERKIN, Sec.-Lt. K., Y. & L.

WHITTAKER, H.

Owing to change of Secretaries, it has been impossible to compile the full list of those members who joined H.M. Forces &c.

SKIPTON

Members who Joined the Forces

Anslow, W.
Armstrong, W.
Bateman, Major, 1/6 West Riding
Bell, Pte. W., R.A.S.C. (M.T.)
Bishop, L.-Cpl. W E.,2/7 Blk. Wh.
Bishop, Steve
Borrison, R.
Broughton, T.
Butler, C. F.
Carson, T.
Chapman, J.
Chapman, T.
Clark, Pte. A., 1/6 West Riding
Clark, C.Q.M.S. Art., 1/6 W.R.
Clark, Cpl. T., 3 West Riding
Cumberland, C.Q.M.S. R. 1/6 W. R.
Curl, C.
Darnbrook, S.
Duckett, Sec.-Lt. R., West Yorks.
Fields, Sgt. P., 1/6 West Riding
Fletcher, W.
Friend, Pte. E., 1/6 West Riding
Gallagher, F.
Gemmell, Pte. C., 26 D.L.I.
Gill, F.
Graham, J.
Green, A.
Hewitt, E.
Holmes, Pte. F., 1/6 West Riding
Horne, Sig. C., West Yorks.
Horner, C.S.M. G. H , 1/6 West R.
Jennings, W.
Lambert, Sgt. A., 1/6 West Riding
Lawson, W.
Macefield, P.
McIntyre, J.
Metcalf, A.
Mooney, Sec.-Lt. S., 1/6 West Rdg.
Mooney, Pte. T., 1/6 West Riding
Morgan, T.
Russell, D.
Russell, J. W.
Slingsby, Lt. P., R.A.S.C.
Soulsby, H. L.
Smith, H.
Stephenson, Cpl. P., 1/6 West Rd.
Thornton, F.
Thwaites, C.
Tindall, Cpl. T., K R.R.
Tindall, H.
Turner, Pte. R., 1/6 West Riding
Walker, W.
Webster, Sgt. J., 1/6 West Riding
Wellock, Pte. W., Royal Scots
Whitaker, R.
Willan, J.
Windle, Sec.-Lt. M., 7 D.L.I.

The Fallen

Armstrong, W.
Bishop, S.
Broughton, T.
Butler, C. F.
Carson, T.
Chapman, J.
Fletcher, W.
Gallagher, F.
Gill, F.
Jennings, W.
Macefield, P.
McIntyre, J.
Russell, J. W.
Russell, D.
Thornton, F.
Tindall, H.
Whitaker, R.
Willan, J.

Honours

Bateman, Major, D.S.O.
Clark, C.Q.M.S. Arthur, Croix de Guerre, M.S.M.
Duckett, Sec.-Lt. R., M.C.
Fields, Sgt. P., M.M., M.S.M.
Horner, C.S.M. G. H., mentioned in despatches
Lambert, Sgt. A., M.M.
Webster, Sgt. J., M.M.
Windle, Sec.-Lt. M., M.C.

BISHOP, S.
Private 1/6th West Riding Regiment
Killed in action July 18th 1915
Skipton R.F.C.

BROUGHTON, T. D.
2nd Lieutenant King's Own Yorkshire Light Infantry
Died of wounds in hospital April 1917
Skipton R.F.C.

BUTLER, C. F.
2nd Lieutenant 112th Brigade Royal Field Artillery
Died of wounds June 8th 1918
Skipton R.F.C.

CARSON, T.
Lieutenant West Riding Regiment
Missing Jan. 4th 1916
Skipton F.C.

CHAPMAN, J.
Lance-Corporal 2/6 Duke of Wellington's West Riding Regiment
Missing presumed killed at Bullecourt May 3rd 1917
Skipton R.F.C.

DAVIES, HAROLD
Lance-Sergeant 2/6th Duke of Wellington's West Riding Regiment
Killed on the Cambrai Front November 26th 1917
Skipton R.F.C.

FLETCHER, G. W.
Gunner 122nd Siege Battery Royal Garrison Artillery
Killed at Arras April 4th 1917
Skipton R F.C.

GILL, F.
2nd Lieutenant West Riding Regiment
Killed in action 1917
Skipton R.F.C.

JENNINGS, B. S.
Lieutenant 9th West Yorkshire Regiment
Died in the Dardenelles November 6th 1915
Skipton R.F.C.

MACEFIELD, PERCY E.
Private 2/6th Manchester Regiment
Killed in France October 7th 1917
Skipton R.F.C.

McINTYRE, J. C.
Lieutenant Yorkshire Regiment
Severely wounded and taken prisoner at Loos September 1915
Died at Seclin, Germany, October 1915
Skipton R.F.C.

PRESTON, P. C.
Captain
Killed in action October 12th 1915
Skipton R.F.C.

RUSSELL, D.
Private 1/6th West Riding Regiment
Died of wounds
Skipton R.F.C.

SUGDEN, HAROLD
Private 1/4th Northumberland Fusiliers
Posted missing May 27th 1918
Skipton R.F.C.

THORNTON, F.
Private 1/6 West Riding Regiment
Died of wounds August 24th 1915
Skipton R.F.C.

WHITTAKER, R. D.
Private 1/6 Duke of Wellington's West Riding Regiment
Killed in action February 28th 1918
Skipton R.F.C.

WILLAN, JOHN WILSON
Lance-Corporal 1/6th Duke of Wellington's Regiment
(Machine Gun Section)
Died of gas poisoning Ypres December 20th 1915
Skipton R.F.C.

SKIPTON GRAMMAR SCHOOL

Members who Joined the Forces

Ashton, R., Wireless Oper., R.N.
Binns, A.
Butler, Sec.-Lt. C. F., R.F.A.
Caw, Pte. H. F., 1 High. Cyc. Batt.
Chapman, A. S., Inns Court O.T.C.
Dickey, Sec.-Lt. J P. Y., 10 Lc. F.
Driver, L.-Cpl. E. O., Training Rs.
Fernsby, Sgt. R., Leicester Regt.
Foulds, J.
Garside, Sec.-Lt. B., West Riding
Hanson, L.-Cpl. T. H., West Yks.
Jowett, Sec.-Lt. P., 8 West Yks.
Lawson, Cpl. W., 6 West Riding
Moore, Pte. R., 6 West Riding
Pickles, Sig. R. H.
Rodwell, Sec.-Lt. W. A., 20D.L.I.
Rogers, W. A.
Rushforth, Cdt. C. H. F., R.A.F.
Slane, T. S., Stretcher Bearer, R.N.S.B.R.
Smallpage, 2/A.M. N. R., R.A.F.
Stansfield, Pte. V., Training Res.
Sugden, Pte. H., Training Res.
Thomson, Cdt. J., R.A.F.
Tindall, Rfn. H., K.R.R.
Tindall, Rfn. G. E., K.R.R.
Townsend, Sec.-Lt. L. C., R.A.F.
Walker, Seaman R., R.N.
Whalley, Pte. W., Leicester Regt.
Wilson, Lt. L., R.A.F.
Woodward, Pte. H., Liverpool Sc.

The Fallen

Butler, C. F.   Caw, H. F.   Rodwell, W. A.
          Sugden, H.   Tindall, H.

Honours

Jowett, P., M.C.

CAW, H. F.
Corporal 16th Highland Light Infantry
Killed September 15th 1917
Skipton Grammar School

RODWELL, WILLIAM ALBERT, M.C.
2nd Lieutenant 171st Tunnelling Corps Royal Engineers
Skipton Grammar School

TINDALL, H.
Rifleman King's Royal Rifle Corps
Killed in action September 15th 1916
Skipton Grammar School

WAKEFIELD

Members who Joined the Forces

ANDERSON, Lt. A. E. P., R.F.A.
ANDERSON, Sec.-Lt. R. O., 14 Y. & L.
ANGUS, Lt. A. M., Gordon H.
APPLEYARD, Lt. W., 6 Yorks. Regt.
ARMITAGE, Capt. A. W., 12 K.O.Y.L.I.
ASPINWALL, Capt. G. R., 10 W.Y.
BALME, R.Q.M.S., F. R., 7 H.L.I.
BATES, Sec.-Lt. J. H., 1/4 K.O.Y.L.I.
BATTY, Sap. N., R.E., I W.T.
BEAUMONT, Major G., 2/4 K.O.Y.L.I.
BEILBY, S.Q.M.S. A., Q.O.Y.D.
BEST, Sgt. T., 1/4 K.O.Y.L.I.
BIRKINSHAW, Cpl. J. R., R.G.A.
BLAKE, Lt. A. T., D.O. R.E.
BOULBY, L.-Cpl. R., 7 R. Mun. Fus.
BRAMER, Lt. H. L. E., Motor G.C.
BROTHERTON, Col. Sir E. A., Bart 15 West Yorks.
BURKILL, Cpl. E., M.G.C.
BURKILL, Pte. A., K.O.Y.L.I.
BUNT, L.-Cpl. R. J. HOPE, Duke of Cornwall's L.I.
BURTON, Sgt. H. G., 46 Bg. R.F.A.
BYWATER, Pte. H., R.A.M.C.
CARPENTER, Capt. G. T., R.E.
CARTER, Cpl. P., Q.O. Yorks. Dgs.
CATON, Ptc. J., 2/4 K.O.Y.L.I.
CHARLESWORTH, Major T. E., 12 K.O.Y.L.I.
CLAPHAM, Sgt. N., R. Can. Con.
CLARKE, Capt. H. M., French A.C.
CLAYTON, Col. Dr. W. K., R.A.M.C.
COBBY, Cpl. R. F. T., R.G.A.
COCKELL, Pte. E., 1/4 K.O.Y.L.I.
COPE, Tpr. F., Q.O. Yorks. Dgs.
CORRY, Pte. F., 1/4 K.O.Y.L.I.
COULTAS, Sgt. S. R., 21 West Yks.
COUPE, Sig. M., R.G.A. att. R.E.
CROSLAND, Lt. J., M.G.C.
DAWSON, Sec.-Lt. H., R.F.A.
DEY, Pte. F., A.S.C.
DIXON, Lt. O. D., 2 K.O.Y.L.I.
DIXON, Pte. W. D., 9 Manch. Rgt.
DODGSON, Sgt. G., R.E.
DUNNILL, Bd. F., R.F.A.

ELLIS, Cpl. P. T., 1/4 K.O.Y.L.I.
ELLISON, Capt. F. B.
FALLAS, Sap. C., R.E.
FIELDING, A. H., A.S.C.
FINN, Air Mech. P., R.A.F.
FIRTH, Sgt. J. H., R.E.
FIRTH, Capt. J. P., 1/4 K.O.Y.L.I.
FIRTH, Pte. H., A.O.C.
FITZWILLIAM, Col. Earl, K.C.V.O., D.S.O., Ox. & Bucks. L.I.
FORDHAM, Sap. A. W., R.E.
FULLERTON, Sgt. J., 14 London Sc.
GIBSON, Lt. J., 13 West Yorks.
GRACE, L.-Cpl. A., R.F.A.
GRAVETT, Cpl. B., R.G.A.
GREEN, Pte. G. M., 1/4 K.O.Y.L.I.
GREENWOOD, Capt. E. A., A.S.C. (M.T.)
GUDGIN, Sec.-Lt. H. W., 5 K.O.Y.L.I.
HADFIELD, Lt. C., 5 K.O.Y.L.I.
HAIGH, Pte. N., 1/4 K.O.Y.L.I.
HAIGH, Cpl. A., Q.O. Yorks. Dgs.
HAMSHAW, L.-Cpl. H., K.O.Y.L.I.
HARPER, Lt. F. C., R. War. Regt.
HARRIS, Sgt. H. M., 4 K.O.Y.L.I.
HARRIS, Capt. C. L., 7 Canadians
HAWORTH, Sec.-Lt. H. S., 1/4 K.O.Y.L.I.
HEAFIELD, Sgt. S., 1/8 West Yrks.
HEALEY, Pte. B., R.A.M.C., Y.M.B
HEIN, Capt. M. H., 1/5 K.O.Y.L.I.
HEMINGWAY, C.S.M. C., 10 K.O.Y.L.I.
HEPTONSTALL, Pte. W., 1/4 K.O.Y.L.I.
HEPTONSTALL, Capt. R. A., 13 Y. & L.
HIONS, Lt. T. H., 13 Y. & L.
HIRST, Sgt. J. A., Q.O. Yorks. Dgs.
HODGSON, Cl.-Sgt. A., 1/4 K.O Y.L.I.
HOLDSWORTH, Lt. L., R.A.S.C. (M.T.)
HOLLIS, L.-Cpl. G. W., 15 West Y.
HOLMES, Lt. S., R.N.R.
HOPKINS, Bd. H. W., R.F.A.
HUDSON, Capt. J. A., 19 Lancs. Fs.
HUTT, Pte. L. R., R.A.M.C.

WAKEFIELD—continued

Members who Joined the Forces—continued

Jackson, Sec.-Lt. H., West Riding
Jubb, Sgt. G. W., R.A.F.
Kaye, Pte. W., 7 K.O.Y.L.I.
Kilner, Cpl. B., Q.O. Yorks Dgs.
Kilner, Sap. L., R.E.
Kingswell, Capt. F. A., Q.O.Y.D.
Lamb, W. Armstrong
Lancaster, Cpl. J., R.G.A.
Lassey, Gnr. C., R.F.A.
Lawe, Capt. F. W., 13 East Yorks.
Lawe, Lt. T., Lab. Batt.
Lawrence, Lt. C. H., R.A.F.
Lee, Cpl. B. W., M.G.C.
Littlewood, Lt. J. D., West Afric.
Logan, Pte. H., K.O.Y.L.I.
Lumb, Lt. H. F., 1/7 West Riding att. to R.A.F.
Marshall, Rfn. T., K.R.R.
Marshall, Lt. G. W., East Ind. A.
Mason, Sec.-Lt. C., M.G.C.
McPhail, C.E.R.A. E. A., R.N.
Miles, Lt. R. E., R.E.
Milner, Capt. M., Hunts. Cyc Co.
Moore, Pte. R. S., Tank Corps
Naylon, Lt. J. A., A. Cyc. Corps
Naylon, Bug. A., 1/4 K.O.Y.L.I.
Nicholson, Gnr. W. H., R.F.A.
Northern, Dvr. T., R.F.A.
Oates, Lt. R. T., R.F.A.
Osborn, Pte. C. K., 1 Colds. Gds.
Parsons, Sec.-Lt. H., 14 R. Scots
Paterson, Sgt. R. W., 1/4 K.O.Y.L.I.
Pepper, Sec.-Lt. C., 1/8 West Yks.
Pepper, Cpl. J. C., R.G.A.
Perry, C.S.M. R., 1/8 West Yorks.
Pickard, Sec.-Lt. R. L., R.F.A.
Pollard, Capt. Dr. P., R.A.M.C.
Pollard, Sec.-Lt. J., K.O.Y.L.I.
Pollard, Sec.-Lt. G. E. W., 5 K.O.Y.L.I.

Quest, Capt. H., 14 Y. & L.
Randall, Pte. R., A.S.C. (M.T.)
Rhodes, Sig. F. B., R.G.A.
Roebuck, C.Q.M.S. E., K.R.R.
Rutter, Sgt. J. J., 1/4 K.O.Y.L.I.
Salmon, Pte. T., H.L.I.
Scowby, Pte. B. W., H.L.I.
Shippam, Sgt. S. P., 1/4 K.O.Y.L.I.
Sidebottom, Tpr. F. E., Q.O.Y.D.
Siswick, S.M. A., Q.O. Yorks. Dgs.
Siswick, Cpl. J., Sherwood R.Y.
Smallwood, Sec.-Lt. B. W., A.S.C.
Spencer, Sec.-Lt. G., 5 Lancs. Fus.
Stanley, Lt. P. V., A.V.C.
Steele, Cpl. H. G., R.A.M.C.
Stocks, L.-Cpl. W. S., A. Cyc. Co.
Summers, Lt. H. C., R.E.
Sutch, Sec.-Lt. R., R.F.A.
Taylor, Sec.-Lt. H. V., 52 Leic. R.
Taylor, Sec.-Lt. T., R.A.F.
Townend, Cpl. H., R.F.A.
Trenholme, Sgt. J., 1/4 K.O.Y.L.I.
Vernon, Sec.-Lt. F. S., Yorks. Rgt.
Wade, Pte. G., Royal Can. Con.
Wade, Rfn. A. E., 16 K.R.R.
Wagner, Act. C.Q.M.S. C. H., 1/4 K.O.Y.L.I.
Wainwright, Sgt. W. G., R.S.G.
Wainwright, Sgt. S. L., Berks. R.
Waite, Sgt. S., 8 K.O.Y.L.I.
Walstow, Cpl. A., 1 Linc. Regt.
Walton, Gnr. H., R.F.A.
Walton, Cpl. S., 14 Tank Corps.
Watson, Bd. C. F., R.F.A.
Webster, Cpl. T., R.E.
Wilcox, Pte C., K.O.Y.L.I.
Wilman, Lt. E., R.A.F.
Wilson, Gnr. J., R.G.A.
Wright, Col. W. H., Staff Rec. Off.

WAKEFIELD—continued

THE FALLEN

ANDERSON, Sec.-Lt. R. D., 14 Y. & L.
APPLEYARD, Lt. W., 6 Yorks. Regt.
ARMITAGE, Capt. A. W., 12 K.O.Y.L.I.
BATES, Sec.-Lt. J. H., 1/4 K.O.Y.L.I.
BOULBY, L.-Cpl. R., 7 R.Mun. Fus.
BURKILL, Pte. A., K.O.Y.L.I.
COCKELL, Pte. E., 1/4 K.O.Y.L.I.
CORRY, Pte. F., 1/4 K.O.Y.L.I.
DAWSON, Sec.-Lt. H., R.F.A.
DIXON, Lt. O. D., 2 K.O.Y.L.I.
HARRIS, Capt. C. L., 7 Canadians
HAWORTH, Sec.-Lt. H. S., 1/4 K.O.Y.L.I.
HEPTONSTALL, Pte. W., K.O.Y.L.I.
HOLLIS, L.-Cpl. G. W., 15 West Yk.
JUBB, Sgt. G. W., R.A.F.
KAYE, Pte. W., 7 K.O.Y.L.I.
KINGSWELL, Capt. F. A., Rifle Bgd.
LEE, Cpl. B. W., M.G.C.
MARSHALL, Pte. T., K.R.R.
MASON, Sec.-Lt. C., M.G.C.
PARSONS, Sec.-Lt. H., 14 R. Scots
PERRY, C.S.M. R., 1/8 West Yorks.
POLLARD, Sec.-Lt. G. E. W., 5 K.O.Y.L.I.
QUEST, Capt. H., 14 Y. & L.
RUTTER, Sgt. J. J., 1/4 K.O.Y.L.I.
SHIPPAM, Sgt. S. P., 1/4 K.O.Y.L.I.
WAGNER, Cpl. act. C.Q.M.S. C. H. 1/4 K.O.Y.L.I.
WRIGHT, Col. W. H., Staff Rec. Off.
WADE, Rfm. A. E., 16 K.R.R.

HONOURS

BATES, Sec.-Lt. J. H., 1915 Star, mentioned in despatches
BEAUMONT, Major G., M.C. and bar
BEST, Sgt. T., D.C.M. 1915 Star
CARPENTER, Capt. G. T., M.C.
CLAYTON, Col. Dr. W. K., C.M.G., 1915 Star
FIRTH, Sgt. J. H., D.C.M., M.M., Croix de Guerre
FITZWILLIAM, Col. Earl, D.S.O.
GREENWOOD, Capt. E. A., 1915 Star, mentioned in despatches
GUDGIN, Sec.-Lt. H. W., M.M. 1915 Star
HARPER, Lt. F. C., M.C.
HEIN, Capt. M. H., M.C.
MCPHAIL, C.E.R.A. R.N., mentioned in despatches
MILES, Lt. R. E., M.C., 1915 Star
PATERSON, Sgt. R. W., M.M. 1915 Star
POLLARD, Capt. Dr. P., Silver Medal from Italian Government
QUEST, Capt. H., M.C., 1915 Star
Shippam, Sgt. S. P., 1915 Star, mentioned in despatches
WATSON, Bd., C. F. D.C.M., M.M. and bar

ANDERSON, REGINALD DUDLEY BAWDWEN
2nd Lieutenant 14th York and Lancaster Regiment
Reported wounded and missing July 1st 1916, since presumed killed
Wakefield R.F.C

APPLEYARD, WILLIAM
Lieutenant 6th Yorkshire Regiment
Killed at Suvla Bay August 22nd 1915
Wakefield R.F.C.

ARMITAGE, A. W.
Major 8th King's Own Yorkshire Light Infantry
Reported missing October 1st 1916 presumed killed in action
Wakefield R.F.C.

BATES, JOHN HAYES
2nd Lieutenant 1/4th King's Own Yorkshire Light Infantry
Killed in action August 31st 1916
Wakefield R.F.C.

BOULBY, R.
Lance-Corporal 7th Royal Munster Fusiliers
Reported wounded and missing August 16th 1915; later reported killed
Wakefield R.F.C.

BURKILL, A.
Private King's Own Yorkshire Light Infantry
Reported missing April 26th 1918 presumed killed
Wakefield R.F.C.

BURGESS, CYRIL, M.M.
Signaller Royal Horse Artillery
Died in France
Wakefield R.F.C.

COCKELL, ERNEST
Private 1/4th King's Own Yorkshire Light Infantry
Accidentally drowned at Gainsboro' February 19th 1915
Wakefield R.F.C.

CORRY, FRED
Private 1/4th King's Own Yorkshire Light Infantry
Killed in action in France September 16th 1915
Wakefield R.F.C.

DIXON, O. D.
Lieutenant 2nd King's Own Yorkshire Light Infantry
Died of pneumonia November 4th 1918
Wakefield R.F.C.

HARRIS, CLAUDE L.
Captain 7th Canadian Infantry
Killed in action at Vimy Ridge, France, April 9th 1917
Wakefield R.F.C.

HAWORTH, H. STANLEY
Lieutenant 1/4th King's Own Yorkshire Light Infantry
Killed in action August 13th 1916
Wakefield R.F.C.

HOLLIS, GEORGE W.
Lance-Corporal 15th West Yorkshire Regiment (Leeds Pals).
Missing on the Somme July 1st 1916
Wakefield R.F.C.

JUBB, GEORGE WILLIAM
Sergeant Royal Air Force
Died September 5th 1918
Wakefield R.F.C.

KAYE, WILLIE
Private 7th King's Own Yorkshire Light Infantry
Killed April 4th 1918
Wakefield R.F.C.

KINGSWELL, FRANK ALFORD
Lieutenant Queen's Own Yorkshire Dragoons attached Rifle Brigade
Wakefield R.F.C.

LEE, B. W.
Corporal Machine Gun Corps 43rd Brigade
Presumed killed at Delville Wood September 16th 1916
Wakefield R.F.C.

MARSHALL, T.
Private King's Royal Rifles
Killed in action November 20th 1917
Wakefield R.F.C.

MASON, C
2nd Lieutenant Machine Gun Corps
Killed in action at Beaucamp, Cambrai, September 27th 1918
Wakefield R.F.C.

POLLARD, G. E. W.
2nd Lieutenant 5th King's Own Yorkshire Light Infantry
62nd Division
Died of wounds September 3rd 1918
Wakefield R.F.C.

QUEST, HAROLD, M.C.
Captain 14th York and Lancaster Regiment
Killed in action November 3rd 1916
Wakefield R.F.C.

RUTTER, JOHN JAMES
Sergeant 1/4th King's Own Yorkshire Light Infantry
Wounded November 4th 1916   Died September 7th 1918
Wakefield R.F.C.

SHIPPAM, S. P.
Sergeant 1/4th King's Own Yorkshire Light Infantry
Mentioned in despatches January 1st 1916
Killed in action November 24th 1915
Wakefield R.F.C.

WADE, A. E.
Rifleman 16th King's Royal Rifle Corps
Killed July 23rd 1916
Wakefield R.F.C.

WAGNER, CHARLES HAROLD
Corporal acting Quarter-Master-Sergeant 1/4th King's Own Yorkshire
Light Infantry
Killed November 25th 1915
Wakefield R.F.C.

WAKEFIELD GRAMMAR SCHOOL

Members who Joined the Forces

BURGESS, C.
DIXON, O. D.
DIXON, P. E.
DUTTON, V
GIGGAL, H.
HAYWARD, S. P.
HOPPER, H. L.
KILBURN, J.

LUND, W. S.
MASSIE, W. H.
MELLOR, A.
SHACKLETON, A. G.
SHAW, W. J.
SUDBURY, E. R
TRENHOLME, F. C.

The Fallen

BURGESS, Bd. CYRIL, R.H.A., M.M.
DIXON, Lt. O. D., K.O.Y.L.I.

GIGGAL, L.-Cpl. H., Cameron H.

Honours

BURGESS, C., M.M.
DIXON, P. E., M.M.
HAYWARD, S. P., M.C.

HOPPER, H. L., M.C.
SHAW, W. J., M.C.

GIGGAL, HAROLD
Lance-Corporal 5th Cameron Highlanders
Died of wounds March 1918
Wakefield Grammar School

YORK ST. PETER'S SCHOOL

Members who Joined the Forces

BRYNING, Sec.-Lt. W. N., K.O.Y. L.I.
BRYNING, Sec.-Lt. H. L. B., Y.R
CHILMAN, Capt. H. L., R.E.
CHILMAN, Sec.-Lt. K. G., R.F.A.
CLUFF, Lt. D. B., D.L.I.
CROWTHER, Cadet F. B., R.A.F.
DAVEY, Sec.-Lt. H. A., Ind. Army
DOOLEY, Sec.-Lt. J. DE R., Innis. Dragoons
ELLIOTT, Lt. C. H., West Rdg. Rgt.
FERGUSON, Sec.-Lt. J. M., 11 Bengal Lancers
GEORGE, Sec.-Lt. S. P., Royal Sikhs, Indian Army
GREENWOOD, A. B. (civilian prisoner interned in Germany 1914)
HARLAND, Lt. M. H., R.A.F.
HARPLEY, Sec.-Lt. R. A., 5 K.O. Y.L.I., att. M.G.C.
HAYNES, Major W. H., R.A.F., late Yorks. Regt.
JOHNSON, Lt. A. O., R.A.M.C.
JONES, Sec.-Lt. M. R., Inf. Ind. Ay.
MEDHURST, Major C. E. H., R.A.F., Inniskillen Fus.
MILLHOUSE, Lt. G., 11 Yorks. Rgt.
PATTINSON, Sec.-Lt. E. P., 2/5 K.O.Y.L.I.
POWELL, Cadet B., R.A.F.
RADFORD, Lt. A. B., R.A.F.
RAINFORD, Sec.-Lt. R. R., West Riding Regt.
REYNOLDS, Sec.-Lt. G. B. E., 1 K.O.Y.L.I.
RICHARDS, Sec.-Lt. P. A. W., York and Lancs. Regt.
RICHARDSON, Sub-Lt. H., R.N.V.R H.M.S. *Excellent*
SERGEANT, Capt. J. H., Yorks. Regt.
STAINTHORPE, Lt. J. C., R.F.A.
WEST, Sec.-Lt. G. C., 3 Sth. Staffs.
WILLIAMS, Cadet F. G., R.A.F.
WRAY, Pte. W. R., Public Schools
YEOMAN, Lt. W. G., Black Watch

The Fallen

HARPLEY, Sec.-Lt. R. A., K.O.Y. L.I.
HAYNES, Major W. H., R.A.F.
PATTINSON, Sec.-Lt. E. P., K.O.Y. L.I.
REYNOLDS, Sec.-Lt. G. B. E., K.O.Y.L.I.
RICHARDS, Sec.-Lt. P. A. W., York and Lancs. Regt.
WEST, Sec.-Lt. G. C., Sth. Staffs.

Honours

HAYNES, Major W. H., D.S.O.
MEDHURST, Major C. E. H., M.C., O.B.E., twice mentioned in despatches
PATTINSON, Lt. E. P., mentioned in despatches
REYNOLDS, Lt. G. B. E., mentioned in despatches, recommended for the V.C.
SERGEANT, Capt. J. H., M.C. Russian Order of St. Anne

HARPLEY, R. A.
2nd Lieutenant 1/5th King's Own Yorkshire Light Infantry
attached Machine Gun Corps
Killed July 5th 1916
York St. Peter's School R.F.C.

HAYNES, W. H. D.S.O.
Captain 6th Yorkshire Regiment attached Royal Air Force
Killed September 26th 1918
York St. Peter's School R.F.C.

PATTINSON, EDWIN POTTER
Lieutenant 2/5th King's Own Yorkshire Light Infantry
Killed in action May 3rd 1917
York St. Peter's School R.F.C.

REYNOLDS, G. B. E.
2nd Lieutenant 2nd King's Own Yorkshire Light Infantry
Killed in action at Beaumont Hamel November 18th 1916
York St. Peter's School R.F.C.

RICHARDS, PETER AUSTIN WILLMOTT
2nd Lieutenant York and Lancaster Regiment
Killed in action at Thiepval, France, September 10th 1916
York St. Peter's School R.F.C.

WEST, GEORGE CLIFFORD
2nd Lieutenant 3rd South Staffordshire Regiment
Killed in action February 12th 1917
York St. Peter's School R.F.C.

"There are others"

"Lest we forget"

PRO PATRIÂ MORTUI SUNT

Blow out, you bugles, over the rich Dead!
  There's none of these so lonely and poor of old,
But, dying, has made us rarer gifts than gold.
  These laid the world away; poured out the red
Sweet wine of youth; gave up the years to be
  Of work and joy, and that unhoped serene,
That men call age; and those who would have been
  Their sons, they gave, their immortality.

Blow, bugles, blow! They brought us, for our dearth,
  Holiness, lacked so long, and Love, and Pain.
Honour has come back, as a king, to earth.
  And paid his subjects with a royal wage;
And Nobleness walks in our ways again;
  And we have come into our heritage.

—Rupert Brooke

www.ingramcontent.com/pod-product-compliance
Lightning Source LLC
Chambersburg PA
CBHW052045220426
43663CB00012B/2449